Plan & Go | Wonderland Trail

All you need to know to complete the classic circuit of Mount Rainier

Alison Newberry, Matt Sparapani

sandiburg press

Plan & Go | Wonderland Trail

All you need to know to complete the classic circuit of Mount Rainier

Content

Welcome

This book is a detailed guide for anyone intending to hike Mount Rainier National Park's Wonderland Trail (WT). Reading the following chapters will give you all the information needed to plan and execute a successful circumnavigation of the iconic peak. Knowing what to expect on any multi-day backpacking trip is essential to enjoying your time on the trail. The suggestions and advice you find in here will help you prepare well for the incredible trekking experience ahead of you on this true American classic.

This book will provide a thorough explanation of what hiking the Wonderland Trail is like and will help guide you through the permit application process, itinerary options, resupply strategies, and transportation considerations in addition to giving general hiking and backpacking tips. While you will not find a detailed history of the trail or a comprehensive natural history on the geology, flora, and fauna encountered, this guide will provide a clear sense of the character of this amazing trail and get readers excited for the natural beauty and wonders awaiting them in this pristine alpine wilderness.

The beautiful Pacific Northwest is undoubtedly one of the most enchanting natural areas of the United States. Graced with temperate rainforests, stunning coastline, and the unparalleled alpine beauty of the Cascade Range, this outdoor enthusiasts' playground has become a magnet for nature lovers from all over the world. With a string of magnificent volcanic peaks dominating the region, Mount Rainier in central Washington reigns supreme. There's no better way to take in the splendor of this grand mountain than by backpacking 360° around it on Washington's iconic Wonderland Trail. The 93-mile (150km) loop circumnavigates the entire mountain, giving you a nonstop parade of jaw-dropping alpine scenery, all with the mighty 14,410-foot (4,392m) glaciated peak as the backdrop. What more could you ask for?

Wonderland Trail Sign near Longmire

1. Introduction

In 1899, Congress granted Mount Rainier national park status, making it the 5th national park in the United States. Before long, it was determined that a trail encircling the mountain would be necessary for rangers to be able to patrol the parklands and to protect the park's resources. Work began in 1907 to build the trail, and, by 1915, the Wonderland Trail was officially opened. The initial trail ran 130-140 miles and was originally closer to the park's boundaries and much less scenic than the 93-mile trail that runs at higher elevations today. It was used primarily by rangers tasked with the duty of patrolling the park. At such a length, a series of cabins was built along the trail giving rangers a place to sleep for a night or an entire season. The cabin at Indian Henry's Hunting Grounds was built during that time period and is still in use today.

The Mountaineers Club of Seattle became the first group to hike the Wonderland Trail for recreational purposes in August of 1915, but, for many years, the trail was deemed unsuitable for most tourists because of its length and difficulty along certain sections. In the early 1920s, the trail became more popular after being shortened and having improvements made to make it more accessible. During this time period, it was also first dubbed the "Wonderland Trail" by the park's superintendent and was marketed in park advertisements as being "the most glorious trip in the world."

The Boy Scouts of America, especially troops from the Puget Sound area, were early users of the Wonderland Trail. They would practice camping skills and wilderness ethics while also providing a service by making regular improvements to sections of the trail. We encountered one group of scouts who were widening the trail on the southern section near Reflection Lakes, so they continue to be involved to this day. The WT has challenged hikers for over 100 years and has been in continuous use since it was first completed. Its popularity continues to soar. In 2015, the National Park Service received a record number of permit requests to hike the entire loop.

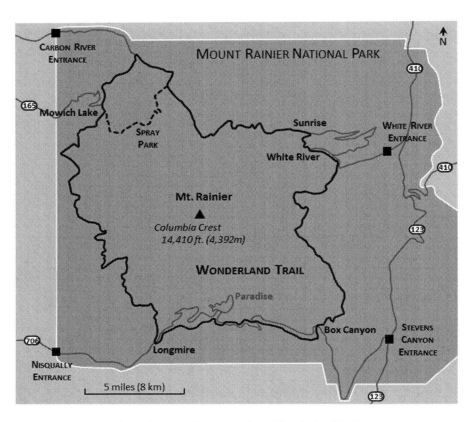

Figure 1 – Overview Map of the Wonderland Trail

We completed the WT in the summer of 2014, one year before the famed trail's centennial birthday. School teachers by day, we are avid travelers during the summer and have been taking extensive trips for the last twenty years. Our trips have evolved a lot over the years, and we focus primarily on designing adventures that allow us to enjoy and appreciate nature, wildlife, and the great outdoors. Although we have always enjoyed day-hiking, long-distance backpacking, at first, seemed out of our reach – too many logistics and potential for problems to wrap our heads around. But, as our interest in hiking, enjoying nature, and trying to document its beauty with our cameras grew, the allure of spending nights and early mornings in glorious settings made us throw caution to the wind and embark on our first backpacking trip in Chile's Torres del Paine National Park.

Before backpacking the WT, most of our trekking had been in other parts of the world. But, after a fantastic experience on some shorter trips in Colorado in 2012, we knew we wanted to attempt some of North America's classic longer treks. The famed Wonderland Trail seemed like the perfect starting point. In addition to the promise of stunning scenery, it offered some conveniences that made the hike particularly appealing. For starters, it is a loop trail, making transportation logistics much easier. We loved the idea of parking our car in one place and hiking back to it at the end. The other big draw was that food cache locations are spaced out evenly along the path. As avid photographers, we tend to carry a lot of extra weight with our camera equipment, and the idea of only having to carry one third of our food and fuel at a time would allow us to bring our heavy cameras while also keeping our backpacks at a manageable weight.

In this Plan & Go guide, we provide a clear picture of everything you will need to successfully plan and execute your own Wonderland experience. Chapter 2 describes the physical challenges of the trail and gives guidance on estimating the time and budget it will take to complete it. Chapter 3 lets you know what to expect regarding trails and navigation, points of interest, weather, camping, water, and safety. The initial estimate of your trail hiking days allows you to prepare for the Long Lead Items of Chapter 4, such as travel plans and transportation considerations for getting to and from Mount Rainier National Park. Important logistical information like planning your itinerary, choosing a starting point, food, resupply, and training is covered in Chapter 5, while Chapter 6 takes a closer look at the gear options suitable for this strenuous hike. Finally, Chapter 7 offers a day-by-day personal account of our experience on the trail in 2014.

As avid travelers, people often ask us what our favorite destination is. Every trip we take is dear to us, and, while we usually say that it is too hard to choose, there are some places that hold a special place in our hearts. The WT is definitely one of them, and we are excited for you as you begin planning your own adventure. We hope this book will enable you to get the most out of your time in this incredible alpine paradise. Happy trails!

Visit *www.PlanAndGoHiking.com* for more information and pictures.

2. Summary of the Challenge

Can you hike the Wonderland Trail? If you love hiking in pristine alpine wilderness, if you have the stamina for a challenging 93-mile (150km), multi-day backpacking adventure, and if you have the mental and physical fortitude to endure 22,000 feet (6,706m) of undulating elevation gain and loss, then the answer is most certainly YES! With the right preparation and attitude, you will find the WT a satisfying challenge that is more than achievable. All you have to do is plan your adventure carefully and go!

a. Requirements

As a whole, the Wonderland Trail is a moderately challenging trail. The footing, for the most part, is non-technical. The trail is well-maintained by the National Park Service and frequently wide enough to allow two hikers to walk side by side. Altitude itself is not a factor, unless you plan to summit Mount Rainier, which is not on the WT and typically not tackled on the same trip. No technical climbing or mountaineering skills are required to navigate the trail, and no special equipment is needed beyond your boots and trekking poles. The gradient on the ascents and descents is lessened by numerous switchbacks. It's never overly steep, even at Panhandle Gap (6,800 ft./2,073m), the highest point on the WT. It is the elevation gain and loss – a constant factor over the 93-mile circuit – that makes the WT a moderate to occasionally difficult challenge.

The Wonderland Trail is a wilderness backpacking experience, which means you must be in sufficient physical condition to carry a fully-loaded backpack for an average of 5-8 hours per day, covering a minimum average distance of 8-12 miles (13-19km). It is important not to underestimate the strength and stamina needed to carry a 30-40+ pound (14-18kg) pack up and down 3000-foot (915m) switchbacks repeatedly, day after day. In addition to a good level of fitness and endurance, you will need a strong back and knees to carry your own food and gear. After a hard day on the trail, camping is the only option for accommodation. You must be able to set up your own tent, know how to use a gas stove, and cook your own meals. The only "luxuries" you will find on the trail are bear poles in each camp for hanging your food and garbage and open-air privies in camps for responding to nature's call.

Mount Rainier is one of the snowiest places on Earth, making the Wonderland Trail accessible only from July to September when the snow has melted sufficiently for safe hiking. This is also the time of year when the weather at Mount Rainier tends to be most pleasant. Having said that, the 14,410-foot (4,392m) glaciated peak is often enshrouded in clouds and known for creating its own weather. You must be prepared to deal with the elements while hiking 360° around it. Heavy rains are common, and summer snowstorms are not unheard of. Temperatures can fluctuate wildly depending on elevation and exposure to wind. Backpacking in less than ideal weather conditions can take its toll on even the most positive hiker.

b. Time

The National Park Service recommends 8-12 days as the average time for completing the entire 93-mile loop. There are many options that allow you to plan your own adventure to match your physical ability and time requirements. There are 18 trailside wilderness camps and 3 frontcountry camps along the route, ranging from as few as 1.9 miles (3km) to as much as 7.3 miles (11.5km) apart from one another. When planning your itinerary, it is important to choose distances between camps that match your age, experience, and fitness level, so that you create a trip you can achieve and appreciate.

In order to have an enjoyable experience with an adequate challenge, start by estimating your days on the trail. Your estimate of trail days (ETD) will help with all your further planning, especially regarding your permit, food, and resupply. Figure 2 below is intended to provide guidance for an initial assessment. Selecting your age and corresponding fitness level will give you an idea of how long it will approximately take you to complete the trail.

For example, a 40-year-old person of average fitness can expect to take roughly 10-12 days to complete the WT at an enjoyable pace.

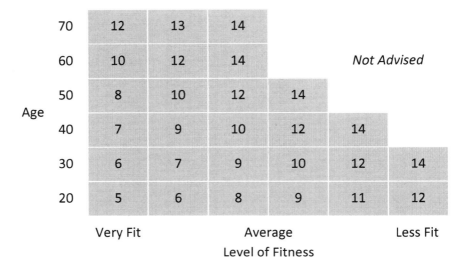

Figure 2 – Estimate of Trail Days on the WT

Once you have determined your ETD, you can calculate your average daily mileage by dividing the total distance of the WT by your ETD:

Average miles per day = 93 miles / ETD

Continuing the above example leads to 93/10 = 9.3 miles per day on average. This might not sound like much, but keep in mind that every horizontal mile is accompanied by a significant gain and loss in elevation. In fact, the 93-mile circuit involves over 22,000 feet of total elevation gain and loss, so this will be a crucial factor to consider in determining the length of your Wonderland experience. You will rarely find yourself hiking on level terrain for even a single mile – there is only up or down! A typical day's hike will usually have you crossing at least one or two of the glacial ridges that descend from Mount Rainier to form its many valleys.

There are other trail-specific factors that will affect your choice as well. The camps are not equidistant from one another, and certain camps may not be available when you secure your permit, so there will necessarily be some longer and some shorter days. How much weight you carry in your backpack, your resupply strategy, weather conditions, and general trail fatigue are also factors to take into consideration. Furthermore, are you the type of hiker who enjoys:

- Hiking at a relaxed pace?
- Taking frequent or long rest breaks?
- Spending time on photography?
- Taking a cool dip in a swimming hole?
- Having down time in camp to read and journal?
- Taking rest days?
- Having extra time for side trips?

If your answer is yes to any of these questions, you will want to plan a more relaxed itinerary to allow extra time to enjoy these activities. If you cannot answer these questions just yet, don't worry. You may only know whether or not you would like to spend more time in certain areas after further research. You can always update your estimate later on.

We encountered hikers of all ages and varying fitness levels throughout our journey. There were families with children as young as 9 years old, couples of all ages, solo hikers, trekking groups, and even a few intrepid trail warriors in their 60s and 70s. As you might guess, the individual amount of time necessary to complete the trail varied quite a bit. We met trekking parties whose itineraries ranged from as little as three days (two ultra-marathoners, who were trail running the WT in three segments of 31 miles each day) to fourteen days (a hiking club traveling shorter distances each day in order to explore side routes). Most groups were completing the WT in 8-10 days. Those that chose to do it in 5-7 days were hiking fast, stopping infrequently, and putting in long hours on the trail each day with little time for rest and relaxation along the route or in camp.

For two hikers of average fitness and backpacking experience in their mid-40s, we found that 12 days to complete the WT was just about perfect. It allowed us to strike a good balance between the average daily distance we needed to cover and actual time spent hiking on the trail each day. As nature photographers, we also wanted the freedom to stop frequently and document the beauty of the WT.

c. Budget

For the most part, hiking the Wonderland Trail is quite affordable. The park service fees associated with walking the trail are negligible. At present, it costs $15 per car to enter Mount Rainier National Park, and, if you are successful in securing an advance permit reservation, the reservation fee is $20 per party for the entire time that you are on the trail. (There is no fee for a walk-up permits.) You will also need to factor in expenses for the food and fuel you will consume during your trip, mailing or delivering caches, transportation to and from Mount Rainier National Park, and accommodation expenses at the beginning and end of your trip.

Depending on your planned hiking mileage on the first day of your trek, it is probably a good idea to spend the evening prior in or near the park to allow time to pick up your permit, drop off food caches, get information about current trail conditions from a ranger station, and to double-check that you have everything you need. There are two options for staying in lodges within the park: the National Park Inn at Longmire and the Paradise Inn at Paradise. In addition, there are several gateway towns outside each of the park's entrances offering many lodging and dining options. Advance reservations are highly recommended during the peak summer season, and most rooms in the area cost a minimum of $100/night and can go up considerably from there.

It is also possible to camp in Mount Rainier's four frontcountry camp-grounds: Cougar Rock (SW), Ohanapecosh (SE), White River (NE), and Mowich Lake (NW). Making advance reservations or arriving early in the morning is necessary for camping within the park, particularly on summer weekends. There are also beautiful National Forest Service campgrounds outside each of the main entrances to the park, which are available only on a first-come, first-served basis.

Other than that, the biggest expenditure will be your transportation costs to and from the park. Currently, Mount Rainier National Park cannot be reached easily by public transportation, so having your own vehicle is a necessity for doing the Wonderland Trail. If you live in the area or within a comfortable driving distance, this is not such a big deal. Simply budget for gas and drive your car to the starting/ending point. But if you are coming from afar, you will need to rent a car to drive yourself to the park. Paying rental fees for a car that sits in a parking lot while you are out on the trail for a week or more is an unfortunate expense, but, if you amortize this cost over the length of your trek, then the access that a rental car provides to one of North America's premiere backpacking routes makes the expense completely worthwhile.

Mount Rainier's Nisqually entrance in the southwest corner of the park is an easy 2-hour drive from either Seattle, Washington, or Portland, Oregon. If you are flying into the area to do this hike, you might compare air fares and rental car rates between the two locations to see where you can get a better deal.

The season for hiking the Wonderland Trail is short, primarily between July and August with a shoulder season of September. The summer months are also prime tourist season in the Pacific Northwest, so shop early to get the best fares on flights.

(i) You might be able to save money on flights, car rental, and accommodation and avoid crowds if you can time your hike for after the Labor Day holiday (the first Monday in September), when most American schools are back in session.

Table 1 below provides a worksheet to help with budgeting for the major expenses involved in hiking the Wonderland Trail. Special treats along the route could include restaurant meals at Longmire, a night off the trail at the National Park Inn at Longmire, and snacks at the Sunrise Day Lodge Snack Bar.

Expense Item	Cost
Flight to/from Seattle or Portland (if needed)	
Transport to/from the park: self-drive or rental car	
Mount Rainier entrance fee	$15/car
Wonderland Trail permit reservation	$20/party
Accommodation before/after hike (if needed)	
Food/gas consumed on trail	
Mailing/delivering food caches along trail	
Treating yourself on the trail	

Table 1 – Expense Overview Worksheet

If this is your first multi-day hiking trip, you might also want to factor in the costs of assembling the necessary gear. Regardless of whether you choose to buy or rent, it is highly recommended to opt for good quality equipment. Functionality and durability are important factors when choosing the right gear, along with comfort level and weight. Going with the cheapest option just to save a few dollars is not advised. You may regret your decision later on when you have to fix a broken shoulder strap halfway through your trip or are freezing at night because of an insufficiently insulated sleeping bag.

Depending on your specific needs and preferences, the expenses for buying a basic kit of decent quality equipment will likely range anywhere from $800 to $1000. Later in the book, we will provide an overview of basic hiking gear items and their features, along with WT-specific recommendations. Those interested in renting gear should check with their local outfitter to find out more about available options and related costs.

3. What to Expect

The Wonderland Trail is a fun, physical challenge that has it all: striking scenery, gargantuan glaciers, rollicking river crossings, thrilling wildlife encounters, spine-tingling suspension bridges, stunning waterfalls, slippery snowfields, serene campsites, and wildflowers galore. This chapter is intended to give you an impression of the conditions and highlights along the trail. This can serve as a guide to choosing your gear and making your preparations. Later, you can compare your thoughts with a gear overview in Chapter 6 and our personal experiences in Chapter 7.

a. Trails & Navigation

Hiking the WT is like walking along the edge of a pie crust. If you look at the profile of elevation gain/loss in Figure 3 below, you will notice that the trail is rarely flat for long stretches. When completing the 93-mile circuit, you will gain and lose over 22,000 feet of elevation.

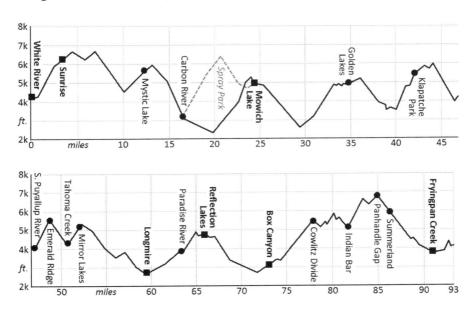

Figure 3 – Wonderland Trail Elevation Profile (counterclockwise direction)

The constant up and down is relentless and the primary challenge on the WT. The good news is that the trails themselves are generally well-maintained, uncrowded, and non-technical. This allows you to pick your head up more often and enjoy the spectacular scenery that surrounds you.

Trail Conditions

The Wonderland Trail alternates between double-wide and single-track trails. As you traverse meadows and forested areas, the path is primarily hard-packed dirt that is fairly smooth and relatively free of roots and rocks that might trip you up. When the path takes you up and over glacial moraines, the path is comprised of gravel, stones, and packed dirt, but still quite firm. With the exception of Panhandle Gap, there is no loose rock or steep inclines/declines that make footing difficult. You will not need to scramble over loose scree and no technical rock climbing skills are required. All you need is a set of sturdy trekking poles to maintain balance and to take the weight off of your knees.

The trail was generally dry and firm when we tackled it in late July and early August, but this is of course dependent on weather. The very next week it rained heavily for several consecutive days which no doubt made the trail conditions more challenging. Although you may have to navigate around a downed tree once in a while, the path is very well maintained overall.

One of the joys of the WT is its constantly varying terrain. On a single day's trek, it is quite possible to climb a moraine, descend through a densely wooded forest, traipse through wildflower-strewn meadows, navigate across a snowfield, cross a raging glacier-fed river by suspension bridge, and stand atop a high ridge with a stunning view of a glacial tarn and the snowy peak of Mount Rainier in the background.

There are a few situations you will encounter along the route worth noting. At several points, you will find yourself ascending or descending monster switchbacks. These switchbacks can go on for a mile or longer at times. For example, between South Mowich River and Golden Lakes, we encountered

33 switchbacks while gaining 2,600 feet in just over 3 miles. What a relief it was to reach camp that afternoon!

Even in late July and early August, you are still likely to encounter snow-fields that obscure the trail. We crossed substantial snowfields at Sunrise, through Seattle and Spray Parks, as well as at Panhandle Gap (between Indian Bar and Summerland). Snowfields can make it challenging to locate the trail. Before crossing a snowfield, try to sight the path across with your eyes or with the aid of binoculars. Use your topographic map and compass to sight land features (peaks, valleys, slopes, etc.) and predict where the trail ought to go in relation to those features. If you are lucky, other hikers will have blazed a trail for you, but there are often multiple footpaths making this option somewhat unreliable.

There are many bridges to cross on the Wonderland Trail. Most are solid constructions that break up the trail, afford a pleasant view up and down stream, and provide a good stop for water and a photo. Take your pack off and enjoy the view. Be aware, however, that there are two impressive suspension bridges at Carbon River and Tahoma Creek (see Figure 4 below) that span spectacular valleys with rivers raging far below. While picturesque from either side, these bridges do sway slightly in the wind and bounce a bit as you cross. If you are afraid of heights, crossing the suspension bridges will be a test of will power. Rest assured, though, they are completely safe. Put your poles away so that both hands are free to grab on to the hand ropes/cables and steady yourself.

Figure 4 – Tahoma Creek Suspension Bridge and South Mowich River Log Bridge

There are at least three bridges along the WT that could potentially be washed out by high waters from glacial melt or rain. These bridges are located in tricky sites for more permanent construction and are made of hewn logs with a makeshift handrail provided on one side only. They are often resting on a base of sand and rock and hover only a few feet or inches above the rushing water below (see Figure 4 above).

When we secured our permit for the WT, the ranger notified us that the bridge over the South Mowich River had recently been washed out and that rangers were hoping to have it repaired within a few days. Bridge repair has to be done by hand as there are no roads and no way to get heavy equipment to the site. By the time we reached the bridge on Day 5 of our trek, we were relieved to find the bridge had been repaired, but the waters were still high. We were advised to cross the bridge early in the morning before the sun hits the glaciers and speeds up the melting process which adds volume to the river. Even so, when we approached the bridge, we found the rushing water was overtopping the bridge and that our boots would certainly get wet. We saw other hikers ahead of us who took off their boots and crossed in water shoes, and so we followed suit. By crossing slowly and holding on to the rickety handrail, we made it past the worst part in only a few steps, but we were not finished yet. We still had to ford two small side streams where there were no bridges by wading through ice cold knee deep water as we struggled to find our footing on the rocky bottom of the stream.

Trailheads

The primary trailheads for hiking the Wonderland Trail are located at:

- White River (via White River Entrance)
- Sunrise (via White River Entrance)
- Mowich Lake (via 165)
- Longmire (via Nisqually Entrance)
- Reflection Lakes (via Nisqually or Stevens Canyon Entrances)
- Box Canyon (via Stevens Canyon Entrance)
- Fryingpan Creek (via White River Entrance)

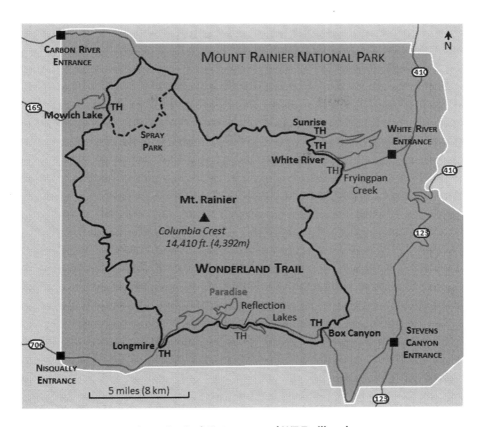

Figure 5 – Park Entrances and WT Trailheads

Each of the trailheads has a parking lot where you are allowed to leave your car for the duration of your hike (vehicle information will be recorded at the ranger station when you pick up/secure your permit). Be aware that, while the other trailheads are frequently visited sites, the parking lots at Box Canyon, Fryingpan Creek, and Reflection Lakes are primarily used by day hikers, leaving your car unattended and more vulnerable at night.

Only White River Campground has camping available directly on-site. All other trailheads will require you to park, pack up your bags, and hit the trail on Day 1 in search of your first permitted campsite, so you will need to plan carefully. It can be difficult and time consuming to drive into the park, check in at the ranger station, drive to your designated trailhead, and pack up your bags before hitting the trail. If your first campsite is several miles down the trail, you could be looking at a late arrival in camp on the first night.

Access to the trail from each of the trailheads is never more than 0.5 miles away from where you park your car. The following lists proximity from parking lot to the WT access point and nearest campsites. Of course, your choice of campsite depends entirely on the route you plan and how many days you budget to complete the 93-mile loop.

White River Campground

Pick up the WT off of Loop D, a few hundred yards from the Picnic and Climbers Parking Lot. If heading counterclockwise, pick up the trail heading north behind the Patrol Cabin and head uphill. If heading clockwise, pick up the trail near the Campfire Circle heading south where you will immediately cross the White River on a series of low, log bridges.

Sunrise

This is a popular day hiking spot. Be sure to arrive early to secure a parking spot in the lot, as the lot frequently overfills in the summer and backs up onto the roadside. Pick up the WT off of the 0.5-mile spur from the parking area; head clockwise (south) to White River (2.1 miles), directly to Sunrise Camp (0.5 miles), or counterclockwise toward Granite Creek (5.1 miles).

Mowich Lake

This is a lesser used trailhead, located in the remote northwest corner of the park. Access is via Highway 165, approximately 33 miles south of Buckley on Mowich Lake Road, a 17-mile long rough gravel road. The campground is less than desirable as it has 10 primitive walk-up only sites with no privacy located on an undifferentiated out-of-use gravel parking lot. The site is not exclusive to WT hikers and is available to campers and day hikers headed to Spray Park. Please note, there is no potable water here, although you can filter from the lake. Your primary reason for stopping at Mowich should be to pick up a cache of food mailed in advance to the Mowich Ranger Station.

Longmire

This is a popular stop located in the southwest corner of the park, 6.5 miles east of the Nisqually Entrance. Longmire has a museum featuring the history of the park, the National Park Inn (featuring a hotel, restaurant, and gift shop), as well as the Wilderness Information Center where you can pick up your permit as well as cache food for your journey. We found it most convenient coming from Seattle to enter the park from the southwest in order to stop here and drop off a cache of food before continuing on to White River. If heading counterclockwise, your first camp is located at Paradise River (3.5 miles away); if clockwise, Pyramid Creek is 3 miles away. If you choose Longmire, we recommend heading counterclockwise. You'll start relatively flat hiking through forest with few views of Mount Rainier but end with the scenic stretch that includes Emerald Ridge and Indian Henry's. Hiking clockwise would produce a somewhat anti-climactic finish.

Reflection Lakes

Located nearly equidistant from Nisqually and Stevens Canyon Entrances (17 and 17.4 miles, respectively), this trailhead provides access to the WT right off Steven Canyon Road on the south side of the national park. If heading counterclockwise, your first camp is located at Maple Creek (4.7 miles away); if clockwise, Paradise River is 2.1 miles away. Reflection Lakes is a popular area for day hiking, however, the parking lot is relatively small. Plan to arrive early in order to secure one of the few parking spots.

Box Canyon

This trailhead is located in the southeast corner of the park on Stevens Canyon Road, 12 miles west of Ohanapecosh, accessed via Highway 123. If heading counterclockwise, your first camp is located at Nickel Creek (1.2 miles away); if clockwise, Maple Creek is 2.4 miles away. If you choose Box Canyon, we recommend heading clockwise to avoid the grueling slog up to the Cowlitz Divide on Day 1. This way would also allow you to finish with Summerland and Indian Bar near the end of your trek.

Fryingpan Creek

Located just 3 miles past the White River Entrance on White River Road, this is another relatively small trailhead with limited parking. Hikers planning on entering the park via the northeast corner and leaving their car parked overnight for several days might want to consider starting from White River or Sunrise instead. Both of these trailheads are only a short drive farther down the road (2.5 and 11 miles, respectively), their parking lots have more capacity, and they are also more regularly frequented. If you still decide to start from Fryingpan Creek, then heading counter-clockwise, your first camp is located at White River (1.4 miles away); if clockwise, Summerland is 4.1 miles away.

Trail Sections

The Wonderland Trail is roughly divided into four main sections which basically correspond to the north, west, south, and east sides of Mount Rainier based on the major access points to the park. The below information is presented in a counterclockwise direction.

White River Campground to Mowich Lake

This stretch of the WT takes you along the northern side of Mount Rainier, passing near the popular Sunrise area, past the Burroughs Mountains to the south, and with spectacular views north down to Berkeley Park. It is possible to follow a spur to the Northern Loop from here (not officially part of the WT but a terrific alternative if you do not get a WT permit). The trail continues along the snout of the Winthrop Glacier, past picturesque Mystic Lake, alongside the mighty Carbon Glacier, and down to the suspension bridge over the roaring Carbon River. While the official WT continues on to Ipsut Creek, most rangers and hikers recommend the traverse across Seattle Park and Spray Park to Eagle's Roost and eventually Mowich Lake. The wildflower bloom here can be spectacular in late July and early August. We were fortunate to hit it at its peak. Fields of glacier lilies are the first to appear after the snow melts.

Mowich Lake to Longmire

This stretch of the WT takes you down the west side of Mount Rainier, crossing the South Mowich River before ascending to the tranquil Golden Lakes. The trail passes through the sought-after Klapatche Park camp before ascending to St. Andrew's Park and back down again to the South Puyallup River. The climb up Emerald Ridge brings you close to Mount Rainier and the Tahoma Glacier before guiding you through Indian Henry's Hunting Grounds with its verdant meadows full of wildflowers before heading back into the forest on your way down to Longmire at 2,780 feet in elevation.

Longmire to Box Canyon

Longmire offers an opportunity to treat yourself to a hot meal at the National Park Inn and/or a cold beer from the park shop before continuing on the WT. This stretch along the southern side of the park is more heavily forested, affording relatively few clear views of Mount Rainier. Highlights include Narada Falls, Reflection Lakes, Martha Falls, Sylvia Falls, and Stevens Creek. Box Canyon is a popular stop for motor tourists and features a welcome flush toilet as well as running water.

Box Canyon to White River Campground

Complete your 360° of Mount Rainier with this stretch of the WT which takes you up the east side of the mountain along the Cowlitz Divide to Indian Bar camp, one of the most impressive vistas along the trail. On a clear day, you have a fantastic view of Mount Rainier's east side and can even see Mount St. Helens off in the distance. The climb up and over Panhandle Gap is one of the more physically demanding days on the WT, but the views make it all worth it. The trail down to Summerland is a feast for the eyes. After Summerland, the trail dips back below tree line as you make your way to White River Campground.

Navigation & Maps

The WT is well-marked with signposts at every camp and major trail junctions, indicating the mileage to the next camp or two in both directions. Once you get a sense of your pace, these are useful for getting a rough idea of when you will arrive at your next camp, not factoring in rest stops, hydration, and time for photography.

There are relatively few intersections with other trails, but all intersections are clearly marked. A quick check with your trail and topo maps will confirm the correct direction to head. The greatest number of intersections with the WT occur around Sunrise, where you will encounter many trails that are popular with day hikers as well. Pay close attention to the signs so that you do not add extra miles to this segment. Between Sunrise and Granite Creek, there are several intersections to be aware of:

- One trail heads to Glacier Basin, a climber's camp for those who intend to summit Rainier.
- A second trail splits north to the Mt. Fremont Lookout, an old firewatch tower.
- A third takes you through Berkeley Park and Grand Park on the Northern Loop, which rejoins the WT at Carbon River.

At Carbon River, the traditional WT continues to Ipsut Creek on the way to Mowich Lake. Many hikers prefer to follow the spur that leads to Cataract Valley camp, through Seattle Park and Spray Park, before reaching Mowich Lake.

On the west side, there are several spur trails off the WT that head to the West Side Road around Klapatche Park (heading to Klapatche Point), the South Puyallup River Trail (heading to Lake George), and the Kautz Creek Trail (at Indian Henry's Hunting Grounds).

Although there are several side trails along the south side, these are well-signed and relatively clear as the WT parallels the Stevens Canyon Road for much of this portion. Be attentive at Box Canyon, as the trail briefly follows the road before crossing the Muddy Fork and soon leaves the pavement heading towards Nickel Creek. Depending on your descent to the road (there are several confusing footpaths), you may or may not walk through a short tunnel before crossing the paved car/pedestrian bridge. Best advice here, follow the trail with a sign that clearly indicates the next camp in your desired direction of travel. Finally, at the Cowlitz Divide, be sure to stay on the WT and avoid the Cowlitz Divide Trail which branches off to the east.

In summary, it is relatively easy to navigate along the WT route, and the path is clearly visible at all times and well-signed. The only difficulty will be when you cross snowfields, but even these sections are relatively short. Proceed with caution following land features and previous hikers' footprints if possible. You should always carry a topographic map and compass in case of an emergency, but in practice you will rarely need the compass on the WT.

We used the Mt. Rainier National Park Hiking Map and Guide, a waterproof topographic map (1:50,000) from Earthwalk Press, in conjunction with the Wilderness Trip Planner Map, which can be found at *http://www.nps.gov* and will be given to you when you pick up your permit. The elevation profile on the back of the topo map was particularly useful for planning our route in advance and for preparing mentally in camp for the next day's segment of the trail. A GPS device is unnecessary, but we enjoyed carrying an altimeter (on a wristwatch) to track elevation gain and loss along the trail.

b. Points of Interest

The Wonderland Trail is full of nonstop amusements that will vie for your attention and provide many pleasant distractions along the way. Be sure to budget time to fully enjoy these points of interest that add to the overall experience and make this a true classic. Beginning at White River Campground and traveling in a counterclockwise direction, here are some of our favorite side trips, swimming holes, and majestic views that you will not want to miss in the order that we encountered them:

Skyscraper Peak: This short side trip 1.3 miles before Granite Creek Camp is a relatively steep climb up to the 7,078-foot summit, but the incredible 360° views of Mount Rainier, Mt. Baker, Grand Park, Berkeley Park, and the Mt. Fremont Lookout will make it all worthwhile. We ditched our heavy packs at the base of the trail and busted out the DSLR camera and hiking tripod for this one.

Mystic Lake: 5.5 miles from Granite Creek, this tranquil lake on the north side of the park just up the trail from Mystic Camp has a lot to offer. In addition to the beautiful reflections of Rainier's northern side, it also provides an opportunity to go for a refreshing swim in a gorgeous setting. A short side trail above the lake leads to a rustic backcountry ranger's cabin with a magnificent view of the mountain and the lake below. If at all possible, try to reserve a spot at the backcountry campsite here to really enjoy all that this lake has to offer.

Old Desolate Pass Tarn: This small, seasonal tarn, just 0.8 miles from Mystic Lake, is a photographer's delight but can be easy to miss even though it is a mere 50 feet off the WT. Look for the small trail sign showing the distance to Mystic Lake at the top of the pass below Old Desolate and follow the small footpath through the bushes to the lake, which is not visible from the trail at all. To get the best reflections of Rainier, try to time your visit when the water is still – either early in the morning or just before sunset. Mosquitoes here are demonic, so be sure to be wearing long sleeves, long pants, and a fresh coating of DEET.

Carbon River Suspension Bridge: This 205-foot-long suspension bridge carries hikers across the tumultuous Carbon River below and provides some fun photo opportunities of the narrow passage to safety.

Seattle and Spray Parks: These subalpine meadows are traversed on an alternate route of the Wonderland Trail between Carbon River and Mowich Lake. The trail here passes through mile after mile of flower-filled

 meadows and quaint meadow streams and is a true feast for the eyes when the flowers are in bloom. Remember not to get too distracted by the countless avalanche lilies, shooting stars, monkey flower, Indian paintbrush, bear grass, and columbine you will see, because the views of Rainier and the surroundings are some of the most impressive anywhere along the entire trail.

Spray Falls: Located on a spur trail 0.25 miles off the Spray Park alternate trail, Spray Falls is an impressive waterfall named for the large volume of spray it generates. Although the full waterfall cannot be seen from the end of the trail, it makes a short, worthy side trip.

Golden Lakes: This is one of the prime (and therefore most requested) backcountry camps along the Wonderland Trail. Not only do the namesake lakes make delightful swimming holes, but the sunset views from the point between tent sites 4 and 5 come along with views all the way to the Olympic Peninsula and Puget Sound. Try to snag a campsite here if at all possible.

Klapatche Park: Another premier WT camp, this one comes with magnificent sunset views of Rainier with a picturesque lake in the foreground. It is definitely worthy of a pit stop if you are not lucky enough to secure a permit for a night's stay here.

St. Andrew's Lake: With its stunning location at almost 6,000 feet in elevation in prime view of Rainier's west side, St. Andrew's Lake makes for a memorable swimming hole, provided you are willing to brave the frigid waters. At less than a mile from Klapatche Park camp, this could make for an excellent sunset destination.

The Collonades: This wall of impressive andesite rock formations is located on the trail on the way to the privy at South Puyallup Camp. Even if you are not staying at this campsite, it is definitely worth the short side trip off the WT to see them.

Emerald Ridge: This beautiful, emerald green meadow at an elevation of 5,600 feet is known for its profuse blossoms and amazing views of Rainier and Tahoma Glacier. Be sure to take the small side trail up to the knoll above the WT for commanding views of the whole area.

Tahoma Creek Suspension Bridge: Hanging 165 feet above raging Tahoma Creek and stretching a whopping 200 feet to the other side, you will definitely want to pull the camera out for photographs of this memorable bridge crossing.

Mirror Lakes: A signpost on the Wonderland Trail marks this side trip to Mirror Lakes. We ditched our heavy packs for the 0.7-mile hike to this pair of scenic backcountry lakes. Be aware, the trail is very flat and can be quite soggy, making it potentially difficult to traverse after heavy rains. If passable, it will take you through beautiful meadows which were in full bloom when we were there in early August. We spent a lot of time photographing the spectacular scenery with Rainier in the background. The trail is only maintained to the first Mirror Lake where magnificent reflections of Rainier await. We bushwhacked our way to the second Mirror Lake but did not find it nearly as photogenic as the first. It is also possible to continue on an unmaintained trail to Pyramid Peak.

Indian Henry Hunting Grounds and Patrol Cabin: Be sure to stop at the Indian Henry Patrol Cabin just 0.2 miles past the Mirror Lakes spur to see the oldest cabin still in use today by the park service. Built by the Civilian Conservation Corp in 1915, its location in the middle of the meadows named after Indian Henry, a well-known Native American who used the area as his hunting grounds, makes us want to quit our day jobs and apply to be park service rangers just for the opportunity to stay there.

Narada Falls: This bridal veil-style falls, dropping 168 feet over a basalt cliff, is a must-see waterfall on the WT. A short side trip off the trail, Narada Falls is about a mile from Paradise River camp. When taking photographs, be careful to watch for spray on your lens.

Reflection Lakes: At the southern end of the park, the Wonderland Trail skirts the edge of Reflection Lakes, one of the most famous spots to photograph Mount Rainier in the park. The WT parallels the park highway here, and a nearby parking lot means you will be competing with day users to get that postcard-perfect shot. Aim to be here as close to dawn or dusk as possible to get waters calm enough to produce the reflections you are after.

Martha Falls: This trailside waterfall is a highlight of the southern section of the trail, but we found the lighting to be a bit tricky. Hope for an overcast day for the best photography.

Sylvia Falls: Sylvia Falls is 2.9 miles east of Reflection Lakes and makes another interesting diversion on this section of the WT. Though pretty, its location in deep forest and its vantage point on a steep slope make it a challenge to photograph.

The Views along the Cowlitz Divide to Indian Bar Camp: After a grueling 2,500-foot climb over 3 miles, you will rejoice at the amazing views of Mt. Rainier's southeast side from the Cowlitz Divide. Be sure to allow for time to stop and smell the flowers as you traverse the meadows along  this gorgeous section of the Wonderland Trail.

Indian Bar Camp: This amazing backcountry camp above the Indian Bar Valley is often described as being one of the best spots to pitch a tent in North America. Cross your fingers that you will be lucky enough to enjoy it with an overnight stay. It doesn't get much more idyllic than this. Snag site #2 if you can get it!

Panhandle Gap: At 6,800 feet, Panhandle Gap marks the highest elevation point on the WT. To reach it, you will cross the permanent snowfields of Ohanapecosh Park, which, at certain times, can be treacherous, but the rewarding views of Fryingpan Glacier and Mount St. Helens behind you and the Emmons Glacier, a seasonal turquoise lake, and Summerland camp far off in the distance ahead are an excellent payoff for your efforts.

Summerland Camp: Located only 4.5 miles from Indian Bar campsite, many people choose to stay at only one of these two camps, but we highly recommend trying to reserve both. You can take your time getting to Panhandle Gap, exploring off-trail at Ohanapecosh Park, and taking in the gorgeous scenery on the way into camp. It is almost guaranteed that you will see plump marmots frolicking about, and the chance of getting a sunrise shot of alpenglow on Rainier's eastern side is enough to make any nature photographer swoon.

c. Weather

Due to the large amount of snowfall that Mount Rainier National Park receives annually (upwards of 700 inches per season), the Wonderland Trail is largely inaccessible until late July. Snow covers much of the trail until late June and early July when the melt is at its highest. Even so, you will likely encounter patches of snow and large snowfields obscuring the path at higher elevations in late July and early August. Although extreme care should be taken in crossing any snowfields, crampons are generally unnecessary for completing the Wonderland Trail in late July and August.

The peak season for hiking the WT is from late July into September, so the window is relatively narrow. Rain is always a possibility, although late summer is generally dry in the Pacific Northwest. July and August receive the least amount of days with measurable precipitation throughout the year. Nevertheless, it is essential to carry proper rain gear and to ensure that your tent is properly waterproofed. As a general rule, the east side of Mount Rainier sees less precipitation than the west side. In effect, the mountain shields weather coming from the west and essentially creates its own weather patterns.

We were fortunate to have experienced 12 days of near-perfect weather, only needing to pull out our rain gear for a brief 15 minutes on just one day of our trek. By contrast, folks we met on the trail said that it had rained periodically for several days just before we started. The week following our trip, during the second week of August, it rained cats and dogs for three consecutive days, completely soaking all WT hikers and their gear and preventing any views of the mountain for days on end. Many waterlogged and disheartened hikers were forced off the trail.

Temperature

The most important measure in deciding what kind of clothing to bring is the expected temperature. Table 2 below gives the average temperatures for the Visitors Centers at Paradise and Longmire, and it also provides a general idea of the temperature ranges on the WT. Keep in mind that you will be changing elevation constantly as you hike, fluctuating from as low as 2,400 ft. (Ipsut Creek) to as high as 6,800 ft. (Panhandle Gap). In order to estimate temperatures along the trail, it is useful to use a lapse rate. As a rule of thumb, deduct 5°F per every 1,000 ft. or 3°C per every 300m of gain in altitude in the respective month you are planning your trip.

Month	Paradise (5,400 ft./1,646m)		Longmire (2,762 ft./842m)	
	°F (low/high)	°C (low/high)	°F (low/high)	°C (low/high)
January	21 / 33	-6 / 1	24 / 36	-4 / 2
February	22 / 35	-6 / 2	26 / 40	-3 / 4
March	22 / 37	-6 / 3	28 / 44	-2 / 7
April	27 / 44	-3 / 7	32 / 53	0 / 12
May	32 / 50	0 / 10	37 / 62	3 / 17
June	44 / 56	7 / 14	43 / 66	6 / 19
July	44 / 64	7 / 18	47 / 75	8 / 24
August	43 / 63	6 / 17	47 / 74	8 / 23
September	39 / 57	4 / 14	43 / 68	6 / 20
October	33 / 48	1 / 9	38 / 57	3 / 14
November	37 / 41	3 / 5	31 / 45	-1 / 7
December	22 / 34	-6 / 1	28 / 39	-2 / 4

Source: Adapted from http://www.nps.gov/mora/planyourvisit/weather.htm

Table 2 – Average Monthly Temperatures at Mt. Rainier

Daytime high temperatures average from mid-60s to mid-70s °F depending on your elevation. Nighttime temperatures can dip as low as 40°F (4°C) at the higher elevations. Dressing in layers is always the wise approach to handling temperature fluctuation out on the trail. See Section 6a *Clothing* for more specific advice on how to dress for the changing temperatures. While we carried a warm hat and gloves, we typically only wore these in camp at night at the higher elevations to conserve heat.

Water along the Wonderland Trail in tarns, lakes, and rivers is glacier-fed and will still be quite cold even in August. Bear this in mind when washing dishes and clothing and if you plan to do any swimming. It is not uncommon to see snow at the edges of mountain lakes, so even sticking your toes in the water to cool your feet will feel quite refreshing, to say the least.

Precipitation

Weather along the Wonderland Trail can be unpredictable, so it is important to be prepared for rapidly changing conditions. Weather at Mount Rainier is typically cold and wet. Although July and August tend to be the sunniest and driest months, rain is always a possibility, so keep your rain gear handy in your front pouch or at the top of our pack, along with your waterproof pack cover, unless you opt for an internal dry bag.

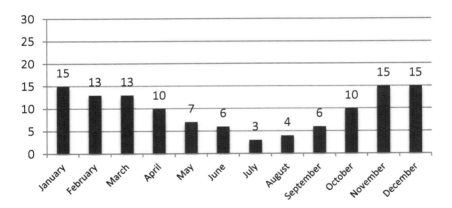

Source: http://www.yr.no/place/United_States/Washington/Mount_Rainier_National_Park/statistics.html

Figure 6 – Average Days with Precipitation per Month

The amount of rain can vary from a brief downpour to a light drizzle over hours. As clouds start to form, it is good to get your light rain jacket readily available at the top of your pack.

> **!** Remember, when seeking shelter during a thunderstorm, move away from freestanding trees and place your pack and other metal

objects at a distance. Avoid peaks and passes and stay low to the ground among scattered boulders or trees.

If you experience heavy rainfall, be aware that bridges along the WT could wash out, making river crossings potentially dangerous and impassable. If park service crews have not repaired the bridge by the time you arrive, proceed with caution. It may be wise to wait until other hikers arrive and cross with them or delay crossing until the waters have receded.

d. Camping

Camping is the only option for accommodation on the Wonderland Trail. There are 18 backcountry wilderness camps and 3 frontcountry sites scattered along the trail, plus 2 additional camps on the Spray Park alternate route (Cataract Valley and Eagle's Roost). Most camps are small but pleasant. Several of them are located in stunning locations, and all have easy access to fresh water. Table 3 below lists each of the camps, the number of individual and group sites, as well as their respective elevation.

Camp	Individual Sites	Group Sites	Elevation in Feet
White River Campgr.*	4	-	4,400
Sunrise Camp	8	2	6,245
Granite Creek	3	1	5,765
Mystic Camp	7	1	5,570
Dick Creek	2	-	4,185
Carbon River	4	1	3,195
Ipsut Creek	12	1	2,360
Cataract Valley	6	1	4,620
Eagle's Roost	7	-	4,885
Mowich Lake*	10	3	4,929
South Mowich River	3	1	2,605
Golden Lakes	5	1	5,130
North Puyallup River	3	1	3,750
Klapatche Park	4	-	5,515

South Puyallup River	4	1	4,000
Devil's Dream	7	1	5,060
Pyramid Creek	3	-	3,765
Cougar Rock Campgr.*	173	5	3,180
Paradise River	3	1	3,805
Maple Creek	4	1	2,815
Nickel Creek	3	1	3,385
Indian Bar	4	1	5,120
Summerland	5	1	5,940

* Frontcountry campsites: White River and Mowich Lake are part of WT permit system; Cougar Rock is a short distance off the WT and requires a separate fee and reservation via Recreation.gov website.

Table 3 – Designated Camps along the WT

Regulations

Camping along the WT is only permitted at the above listed camps. Each backcountry camp has 2-8 designated, flat sites where you set up your tent. Each camp also has either a primitive pit toilet or a composting toilet, a bear pole for hanging your food, garbage, and scented items, as well as a water source relatively close by. Individual sites can accommodate 1-5 people and hold a maximum of 2 tents. Parties of 6-12 people needing 3-5 tents must reserve a group site.

[!] Keep in mind that not every camp has a group site, so this will limit your options as you plan your itinerary. Parties larger than 12 people are not permitted on the WT!

The National Park Service has several important regulations worth recalling:

- Destroying or disturbing any natural feature in Mount Rainier National Park is prohibited as well as feeding or disturbing wildlife.
- Avoid polluting or contaminating any water source by using soap to bathe or to wash your dishes.

- Carry a collapsible bucket so you can rinse your body and your dishes at least 200 feet (60m) from any water source.
- LEAVE NO TRACE. You must pack out all of your garbage.
- Do not throw any trash in the pit toilets and never leave any manmade items in the wilderness.
- Police your camp before you leave in the morning and try to leave it cleaner than when you arrived.
- You must use a gas-burning stove to cook your meals on the WT. Campfires are strictly prohibited!

⚠ Remember that you are camping in bear country on the Wonderland Trail. Keep a clean camp to prevent any unwanted visitors. This is not only for your safety but also for the well-being of your fellow hikers and the animals. Never leave your food unattended, even for a short while. Always hang your food, garbage, and scented items at night using the bear poles provided at each camp.

We encountered 5 bears on the WT, including a mother and two cubs in camp at Mystic Lake. Bears are incredibly quiet as they forage for food and can appear without warning. There is no reason to fear them as long as you respect them.

Choosing a Campsite

As part of the permit process, you must list the backcountry camps where you intend to camp each night. If your permit reservation application is successful, you will receive a confirmation letter detailing your itinerary. It is important to check your permit carefully to make sure that the camps listed are correct. If there is a mistake, contact the Longmire Wilderness Information Center to see if it can be altered. If a change is not possible at that time, it is worth inquiring again in person when you pick up your actual permit. You will now be within the window for walk-up permits (i.e., one day prior to your departure), and camps that were previously full may now have become available for reservation.

(i) Be aware that most campsites on the Wonderland Trail are set in forested areas. The upside to this is that you are better protected from the elements; the downside is that the sites generally do not come with the views that you may be hoping for. Keep this in mind out on the trail. There is generally no rush to get to camp. Take your time and savor the incredible views and scenery along the route as there is not a lot to see in the camps themselves.

Tent sites in the backcountry camps are available to permit holders on a first-come, first-served basis. Upon arrival in a camp, check out the unoccupied sites and pick the one that best suits you. After setting up your tent, be sure to attach your permit to your tent so any rangers stopping by to check can easily see that you are where you are supposed to be.

Figure 7 – Attaching Permit to Tent and Pit Toilet

Your permit guarantees you a spot in each camp, so you do not need to worry about arriving late and finding no sites available. If, by chance, this were to happen, tent sites are generally large enough to accommodate additional tents. You should double-check permits with other campers to determine where the mistake lies and, if necessary, double up for the night with an agreeable party. We never encountered this problem on our trip.

Larger camps have a designated group site for parties of 6-12 hikers. Do not choose this site unless your permit specifically indicates that this is your camp. If this is the case, you must set your tent up in the group site and not in one of the individual sites. We were assigned the group site at Golden

Lakes and were pleasantly surprised that the impressively large site was reserved for us alone. Score!

| ! | It is worth knowing that it is possible to change your itinerary while out on the trail. If you encounter a backcountry ranger with a walkie-talkie, they can check in at the permit office to check on alternate site availability. |

We kept hearing that Devil's Dream was mosquito-infested and hoped to change to Pyramid Creek a few miles down the trail. A few days before, the ranger at Golden Lakes contacted the permit office for us, changed our reservation, and indicated the new camp on our permit. Mystic Lake, Mowich Lake, Golden Lakes, and Summerland have backcountry ranger cabins/camps where changes could potentially be made. The frontcountry ranger stations at Longmire and Sunrise also provide an opportunity to make adjustments to your itinerary if necessary.

e. Water

Water is readily available along the trail. You will frequently cross streams and rivers flowing with the glacial melt waters off of Mount Rainier, and there are also numerous lakes and tarns where it is possible to draw water.

Each backcountry campsite is located within close proximity to a fresh water source, but this does not always mean that the source is located immediately in the camp. Sometimes, it could be as much as a quarter mile away. A good strategy to avoid having to backtrack to find water is to talk to other hikers you pass along the trail and inquire about the location of water sources at the various camps. If you know that the water source is farther away and that you will pass it on your approach to camp, you may want to stop for water on the way there. Keep your filter and water bladder close to the top of your pack.

While the quality of the water is generally good, it is always necessary to treat the water before drinking it by filtering, boiling, or treating it with iodine or water purification tablets. When water sources are found close to camps, try to draw upstream of the campsites to avoid consuming any water that might have human contamination. Since the water sources are glacier-fed, there can be a lot

of sediment present, particularly in the larger rivers coming right off the glaciers, which could potentially clog your filter. To prevent this, look for water sources that are clear and avoid those that appear milky from glacial runoff.

Any water you find should be refreshingly cool for drinking and will provide instant relief on a hot day. Several lakes along the trail make for refreshing swimming holes, but the chilly temperatures may be a roadblock for some. Because some of these lakes are also the main source of water for the camp, it is important not to use any soap products in them. If you feel soap is necessary, make sure it is biodegradable, fill a collapsible bucket, and carry it a minimum distance of 200 feet away from the water source to do your washing. The same holds true for washing clothing and camp dishes.

f. Flora & Fauna

One of the elements that make hiking the WT such an enchanting experience is that the landscape in front of you is constantly changing. One moment you are hiking through a cool and shady subalpine forest, the next you are strolling through a mountain meadow strewn with wildflowers in bright sunlight. As you cross rivers or ascend to high ridges, you will gain views of Mount Rainier's spectacular glaciers. If you are lucky, you may catch sight of some of the park's elusive birds and mammals. In high summer, you are quite likely to spy a black bear eating blueberries along the way. The constant change of elevations gives you plenty of opportunities to see how the vegetation changes as you pass in and out of different eco-zones over the course of each day.

Plants

Mount Rainier National Park is world-famous for its magnificent wildflower displays, and the Wonderland Trail passes through several subalpine meadows (called *parks* in the Pacific Northwest) where you can witness this amazing spectacle for yourself. There's nothing quite like hiking past a carpet full of colorful blooms with the magnificent peak of Mount Rainier serving as a backdrop. Seattle Park, Spray Park, St. Andrew's Park, Emerald Ridge, Indian Henry's, Indian Bar, Ohanapecosh Park, and Summerland Camp each have the potential to be mind-blowingly gorgeous. Bloom times vary each year depending on rainfall and temperatures, but late July and early August tend to be the most reliable times to see the spectacles. If you manage to catch the wildflowers at their peak, you can expect to see fields exploding with bear grass, avalanche lilies, Indian paintbrush, columbine, monkey flower, shooting stars, gentian, western anemone (nicknamed "hippies on sticks"), and lupine. Please be especially careful to stay on the trail when traveling through these fragile areas to help protect them for all to enjoy.

Figure 8 – Monkey Flower and "Hippies on Sticks"

Over half of Mount Rainier National Park is forested. Along the WT, you will pass through sections with impressive stands of trees that add to the beauty and the tranquility of the experience. While you are slogging your way up and down some killer switchbacks or relaxing and catching your breath, it is fun to know a little about the forest surrounding you. Look for western hemlock, Douglas fir, and western red-cedar that are prevalent in the lower elevations. As you climb higher, these give way to western white pine, Alaska yellow cedar, and several species of fir. One concern for hikers is that heavy snows, rainstorms, and melting snow can bring down countless trees over the trail. Trail clean-up keeps the park service busy as they do their best to maintain the WT.

Animals

Animals are a relatively rare sight on the trail. We saw several bears, deer, squirrels, marmots, and a small variety of birds during our trek. Sightings of mountain goats are common around Berkeley and Ohanapecosh Parks. Bear sightings can happen anywhere, but be especially cautious and noisy while hiking through areas with blueberry bushes in fruit. The WT passes through prime bear habitat on the west side of the park, particularly between Golden Lakes and Klapatche Park. If you are hoping to see marmots, you are in luck. Sightings of the cute critters are practically guaranteed in Spray Park, Emerald Ridge, and Summerland. It is possible to see elk, mountain lions, and beaver as well.

Figure 9 – Young Buck and Marmot

g. Safety

In general, the national parks offer one of the safest places to visit in the United States. Crime is virtually non-existent, but unfortunately petty crimes sometimes do occur. Signs at trailheads and in parking lots advise visitors to keep all valuables out of sight when locked in your car. If possible, store anything you are not taking with you on the trail in your trunk, so it is not visible. If your car does not have a trunk, do your best to hide or cover anything that may be attractive to thieves.

Fellow Hikers

Most other hikers you meet will be friendly and of a similar mindset – simply there to enjoy the beauty of nature and the solitude that comes with hiking in remote wilderness. Having said that, it is still advisable to be cautious while on the trail, particularly if hiking alone. If you meet anyone who makes you uncomfortable, try to avoid telling them that you are solo hiking and where you will be camping each night. You might say that your hiking partner is trailing behind you and will catch up shortly or that you forget which camp you will be staying in that night.

Wildlife Encounters

There is plenty of wildlife to see on the Wonderland Trail, including marmots, deer, elk, goats, and black bear. Mountain lions do exist in the

park but are rarely seen. Be sure to make plenty of noise while walking on the trail to warn any bears in the area of your presence. If you do see a bear, keep calm and do not run. Maintain a safe distance and do not approach the bear. Avoid looking the bear in the eye and speak in a
calm voice. If possible, slowly move upwind of the bear to alert it of your presence. Watch for signs of nervous or aggressive behavior, such as the bear lowering its head and swaying it back and forth, flattening its ears,

slapping its paws on the ground, and making growling or clicking sounds with it teeth, as this is a warning that you are too close. Slowly distance yourself from the bear. Wait for the bear to leave the area or give the bear an extremely wide berth as you move around it. Be especially cautious if you see a mother bear with cubs.

Food Storage

For your safety and the safety of those around you, you will need to keep a clean camp to prevent any unwanted visits from bears or rodents. Never leave food unattended and refrain from storing food or scented items in your tent. If possible, cook and eat at least 100 yards (90m) away from your tent. Each camp has a bear pole, making it easy to store all your food in the air and out of reach from animals. Be sure to pack your food and any other items that smell, including all garbage, toiletries, and dishes in a light waterproof bag that will keep everything dry when hanging exposed overnight. If your bag is heavy, it may be a challenge to hoist it up on the bear pole. Consider splitting your supplies into two or more bags to make stashing easier.

Insects

Mosquitoes and bugs will be a constant nuisance on the Wonderland Trail. Be sure to pack lots of bug repellant with a hefty amount of DEET. You will certainly need it!

⚠️ Before using DEET-based repellents, be sure to familiarize yourself with the pros and cons of their application and proper handling instructions.

Fording Rivers

There are a few places along the route where bridges could potentially be washed out by high waters from glacial melt or rain. If you do have to cross rivers, there are a few important safety guidelines worth following: first, unclip the waist and chest straps on your backpack, so that, if you fall in, you could quickly free yourself from your pack; second, use your hiking poles to brace yourself but do not look down at the water as it can become disorienting and throw you off balance; third, cross at a slight diagonal facing upstream and shuffle your feet to feel for hidden rocks and boulders rather than taking big steps. If you are uncomfortable crossing on your own, wait for other, hopefully more experienced hikers to come along the trail and ask to cross with them. You might also consider linking arms with your hiking buddies or other hikers for additional support. Worst-case scenario, wait a sufficient amount of time for the river to recede or seek an alternate route.

Crossing Snowfields

Be aware of a few dangers involved whenever you hike over snow. The risk of *post-holing* (plunging through the snow up to your knee or higher), especially in late summer as the snowfields are melting, is very real. Snow can obscure variation in the terrain below as well as rocks that you would normally avoid if you could see the trail. Where the edges of snowfields meet the unobscured trail is particularly dangerous  as the snow often melts from underneath (below where you are walking) and creates a shelf. This is difficult to impossible to see from your vantage point on the snowfield, and, as you approach the edge of the snowfield, there is a risk of the shelf collapsing and/or of stepping into meltwater and topping your boots. Cold, wet feet can be dealt with, but a sprained knee or ankle could end your trip early.

(i) We were concerned about crossing snowfields before our trip but were advised by park rangers that crampons were unnecessary. While slipping on snow is always a concern, we found that stepping slowly, deliberately, and carefully, as well as digging our heels into the snow and bracing with poles made it possible to traverse snowfields safely.

h. Other Conditions

Wildfires

In recent years, drought has afflicted the Western United States and helped create conditions for wildfire. As recently as 2014, the section of the Wonderland Trail between White River Campground and Sunrise was closed due to a wildfire started by lightning strikes. Hikers were instructed to follow an alternate route via Glacier Basin and Second Burroughs. Many hikers opted to go to the Sunrise Visitor Center and catch a ride to the White River Campground instead.

While you cannot prepare in advance for wildfire, you can take the right precautions. When you pick up your permit, always ask the park ranger about current fire conditions. Once on the trail, ask other hikers you meet about the status of current wildfires. Camps at Mystic Lake, Mowich Lake, Golden Lakes, and Summerland have remote ranger cabins or camps that are staffed by backcountry rangers. They are a good source of up-to-date information while out on the WT.

 Remember, campfires are strictly prohibited in the backcountry of Mount Rainier.

Geohazards

Mount Rainier poses several geohazards that you should be aware of when you hike the Wonderland Trail. It's worth a reminder that Mount Rainier is still technically an active volcano, which, although dormant at present, could erupt again in the future. More importantly, the mountain is covered by 27 glaciers, whose advancement and melting have carved the ridges and valleys that make the terrain along the WT so interesting and challenging. From time to time, including as recently as August 2015, glacial melting triggers large debris flows called *lahars*[1] that send a massive volume of water, mud, boulders, and trees downriver at a rapid pace.

---

[1] The word *lahar* is of Indonesian origin.

The National Park Service advises that you listen for sirens and evacuate to higher ground immediately, especially if you notice any rivers rising rapidly, feel the ground shaking, and/or hear a low rumbling sound coming from upriver. A more frequent concern is that melting glaciers will cause a rise in the river level that could wash out bridges and make river crossings challenging, if not dangerous. Check with the ranger when you pick up your permit to see if there are any current geohazards and/or bridges out along the WT before setting out on the trail.

In turn, Mount Rainier provides one of the best opportunities to see glaciers in the lower 48 states. Be sure to enjoy the spectacular close-up views along the trail of these massive ice flows, especially the Winthrop, Carbon, Tahoma, Fryingpan, and Emmons glaciers. Although the WT does not take you close enough to actually touch a glacier, resist the temptation to go off trail and hike on any glacier, as they can be dangerous and unpredictable, especially without having proper equipment and an experienced guide to lead you.

Figure 10 – Trailside View of Winthrop Glacier

4. Long Lead Items

A cousin of mine, a blacksmith and now a mountaineering guide, once had written on his forge, "Think Sequence," to remind him of the importance of being both orderly and efficient in accomplishing a task with multiple steps. We think of this every time we begin planning for another outdoor adventure. Arranging a multi-day backpacking trip on the Wonderland Trail involves several steps, some requiring more lead time than others. This chapter introduces the most important items that require advance thinking and preparation in order to have a successful and enjoyable journey.

a. Permits & Regulations

A wilderness permit is required to stay in the designated camps along the Wonderland Trail. As the number of campsites is limited, so is the number of available permits. About 70% of the wilderness permits can be reserved in advance, while the remaining 30% are walk-up permits that are issued on a first-come, first-served basis. Those wishing to climb above 10,000 feet or onto any of the glaciers must purchase a separate climbing pass (see National Park Service website for details).

Advance Permit Reservation

Starting March 15 each year, the park accepts permit reservation requests via *fax* or *mail* for the upcoming season through the end of September. Advance reservations may also be requested *in person*, but this option is only available at the Longmire Wilderness Information Center after it opens to the public in late May.

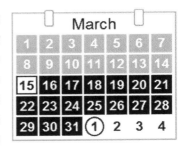

No advance reservation requests are accepted for trips starting after September 30. If you intend to start your hike or climb after this date, you are expected to show up in the park in person and attempt to acquire a first-come, first-served permit.

Application Process

In order to apply for an advance permit, begin by downloading the Mount Rainier's Wilderness Reservation Request Form from the National Park Service website. Fill out the form very carefully with your contact information and your requested itinerary, indicating which camps you want to stay at each night during your trip. (Section 5a *Itinerary* will assist you with carefully planning your route.) There is a non-refundable $20 fee for an advance wilderness permit reservation, so a credit card number must be given on the form. The fee covers up to 12 people in a single group for up to 14 consecutive nights on the trail. The fee is only charged if your application is accepted.

Print out the completed form and either fax *or* mail it to the Mount Rainier National Park Wilderness Information Center (contact information provided in Appendix H) between March 15 and midnight PST March 31. If you prefer, you can also print a blank form and fill it out by hand, in which case the park service recommends using your best handwriting and black ink, especially if then faxing your application. Even though it is technically also possible to deliver your request in person once the Longmire Wilderness Information Center opens to the public in late May, we do not recommend this option. Given the popularity of the WT, all advanced permits will likely have been filled by then.

Getting a permit definitely involves a stroke of good luck. Starting April 1, park staff pull advance permit applications received between March 15 and 31 in a lottery process and try to fill as many permit requests as possible. The order in which requests have been received during the initial application window does not matter. Permit requests arriving on or after April 1 are processed in the order they are received, but only after processing the massive amount of requests received in March.

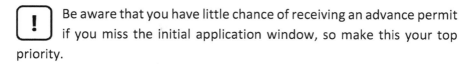 Be aware that you have little chance of receiving an advance permit if you miss the initial application window, so make this your top priority.

Permit Strategy

You can improve your chances of having your permit application fulfilled by indicating that you are willing to accept alternative start dates (you must enter a specified range for the start date) and/or that you are willing to stay at alternative camps if the ones you requested are full. You can also include multiple itineraries in your application by submitting additional forms with your request, changing the choice number, and altering your itinerary. For example, if you want to begin your trek on August 1, you could submit one itinerary for 10 days starting at White River going counterclockwise, a second choice starting at Longmire, a third choice going clockwise from Mowich, etc. By providing multiple itineraries you give the park service flexibility in fulfilling your request. Only submit one application per group, as the park service do their best to remove all duplicate applications.

The Wonderland Trail has become insanely popular in recent years. In 2015, the park service stopped accepting applications in early April due to the overwhelming demand for permits. Allowing the park service staff to have some flexibility while processing your request significantly improves your chances for success and may make all the difference with your application.

Confirmation and Pick Up

If the trail gods smile on your application, you will get a confirmation letter from the park service within a few weeks stating that your permit request has been filled and confirming your exact camping itinerary. If your permit request was not successful, you'll receive a denial letter stating that is has not been filled.

Once your camping itinerary has been confirmed, you are allowed one change at no additional fee, provided the change can be accommodated by the park. Each subsequent change incurs an additional charge of $20.

It is important to know that the confirmation letter is not your permit, it is only a reservation placeholder. You must register and pick up your actual permit at a ranger station in the park <u>before 10:00 AM</u> on the first day of your trip. You can also pick up your permit the day before your departure, but no sooner than that. In the summer, these ranger stations include:

- Longmire Wilderness Information Center; +1 (360) 569-6650
- Jackson Visitor Center at Paradise; +1 (360) 569-6571
- White River Wilderness Information Center at the White River Entrance; +1 (360) 569-6670
- Carbon River Ranger Station located 2.5 miles before the Carbon River Entrance; +1 (360) 829-9639

⚠ If for some reason you are unable to pick up your permit prior to 10am, contact a ranger station to let them know you will be arriving late. Otherwise, your reservations will be forfeited and added to the pool of camps available to hikers seeking walk-up permits.

When picking up your permit, the rangers will ask you to supply the following information:

- Make, model, color, and license plate number of ALL vehicles that will be left overnight anywhere in the park during your trip.
- An emergency contact name and phone number.

Be sure to have all of this information ready when arriving at the ranger station, as your permit will not be issued until you can provide it.

Walk-up Permits

Fortunately, for unlucky people, like us, who receive a denial letter, or folks who simply cannot plan several months in advance, the park service sets aside 30% of the backcountry sites for first-come, first-served walk-up permits. These permits are free of charge but do not become available until one day prior to heading into the wilderness. Since most backcountry camps only have 3-8 campsites in total, this means that only 1 or 2 sites at each camp are held open for people applying in person.

This may not seem like very good odds, but we are here to tell you that the walk-up process can work out in your favor. We had our hearts set on trekking the Wonderland Trail and ultimately did not care where we started or which direction we went, as long as we could have a minimum of 10-11 days to complete it. We decided we would take our chances, fly to Washington State, be as flexible as possible, and ultimately be happy to spend two weeks hiking or backpacking elsewhere if we could not secure a permit.

We visited the Wilderness Information Center at Longmire to apply for our permit in person. We timed our arrival for early morning and crossed our fingers as we walked in. We had our original permit applications with us and showed our ideal itinerary to the helpful ranger. Within a few minutes, she secured all but two of our requested camps. We were able to choose alternate camps for those locations, and the process was done. We couldn't believe our good fortune!

Helpful Tips

We discovered later on the trail that there were several factors that greatly increased our chances that fateful day. The first was that we arrived on a Monday and technically started our Wonderland experience that day by staying overnight in the backcountry camp at White River Campground. (In reality, we just drove ourselves to the campground and spent the night there before hiking the next day.) Avoiding the busy weekend and starting on the slowest day of the week gave us a huge advantage.

Other factors that helped us were the direction we hiked and the length of our itinerary. Traveling counterclockwise tends to be less popular, so we had less competition from other walk-up permit seekers for sites each night. Being on a 12-day pace was another huge advantage. We managed to score reservations for many of the premier camps along the route at the end of our trek, including Indian Bar and Summerland, two of the park's most popular backcountry camps. It would be practically impossible to stay at either of these camps on the first day of a walk-up trip. By initiating a walk-up backcountry wilderness permit, we had unlocked access to the first-come, first-served sites at these sought-after camps. This is because they were far enough from our starting date that they were not yet taken and only available to us and other walk-up permit seekers. This was an incredible advantage, especially given that we were hiking in late July and early August, the Wonderland Trail's peak season.

Regulations

Fires, pets, bicycles, and other wheeled devices are not permitted in the backcountry at Mount Rainier. Although firearms may be possessed or carried in accordance with Washington State law, the use of firearms throughout the park including backcountry areas remains prohibited.

b. Hiking Buddy

While it is certainly possible to hike the Wonderland Trail solo, it is important to fully understand what you are getting yourself into if you choose this option. Unlike other popular long-distance hikes, like the Pacific Crest Trail or the Appalachian Trail, this trail (even at 93 miles) is relatively short and is regulated in such a way as to make trail camaraderie challenging. Each itinerary is unique in length and choice of camps. Once you set out, it is difficult to alter your itinerary. You must stay in the camp for which you are permitted. The result is that you may not simply go with the flow and camp with interesting people you meet along the way. In addition, some hikers are traveling clockwise while others are traveling counterclockwise. We met hikers completing the WT in as few as five days and as long as 14 days. All of these variables make it difficult for the solo hiker to develop and sustain trail friendships if that is part of what you are hoping to find during your journey.

Generally speaking, it is always safer to travel with a hiking buddy in case of emergency. In practice, however, there is enough traffic on any given segment of the WT that you will likely encounter, at least in high season, several hikers each day. There are also several exit points, and you are rarely far from either a ranger cabin or national park road if you are in need of help. That said, having a hiking buddy to share the trail experience with and help carry the weight of food and equipment is always a plus. Most of the hikers we encountered were traveling in pairs, but we also saw several solo hikers as well as hiking groups as big 10. Regardless of your group's size, it may be easiest to plan your own menu and carry your own food to account for different diets, appetites, and food preferences.

Finding the right companion can be a challenging endeavor in itself and should be given thorough thought. The following questions may aid you in your decision-making process when looking for potential candidates:

- Will you be comfortable being around that person 24/7 for the entire duration of your trip?
- Do all of you have somewhat similar fitness levels and hiking experience?
- Do all of you share similar interests and expectations (e.g., taking lots of photos, off-trail relaxing/exploring)?

If you decide to look for a hiking partner, approach people early so they have sufficient time to carefully assess if they are capable of the challenge and whether or not they have the necessary resources available to them. Potential doubts and concerns should be discussed openly and sorted out well before hitting the trail.

c. Travel Arrangements

The beauty of the Wonderland Trail is that it is a loop trail, making the logistics of hiking it much easier compared to a point-to-point trail. Returning to your starting point allows you to leave your car and not have to worry about finding transportation back to it as you would on a point-to-point hike. All of the trailheads (White River, Sunrise, Mowich Lake, Longmire, Reflection Lakes, Box Canyon, and Fryingpan Creek) have a parking lot within half a mile of the WT. The challenge is that there is no public transportation option that will get you into the park.

Mount Rainier National Park's Nisqually Entrance in the southwest corner of the park is 82 miles from Seattle-Tacoma International Airport (SEA), 138 miles from Portland International Airport (PDX), and 137 miles from Yakima Air Terminal (YKM), so renting a car is essential. This makes it difficult to fly in, travel to the park, register and pick up your permit, deal with food caches, and begin the WT all on the same day. You will, therefore, most likely need to factor in an extra day on either end of the trip for travel. Of course, if you already live near Mount Rainier National Park, travel arrangements will be much more straightforward.

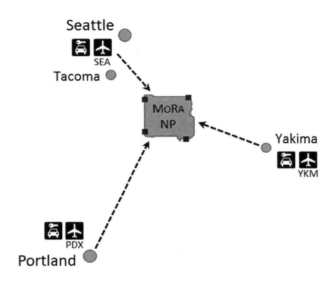

Figure 11 – Overview of Travel Options

d. Trail Shelters

The Wonderland Trail does not offer any commercial shelters along its path, so you will need to be self-sufficient in terms of sleeping. A few of the backcountry campsites offer basic, three-sided stone shelters (see Figure 12 below). Built by the Civilian Conservation Corps (CCC), these rustic shelters provide a roof over your head and an atmospheric place to stay for the night but not much else.

Figure 12 – Indian Bar Stone Shelter

The group shelter at Indian Bar Campground offers a huge stone fireplace and bunks mounted to the stone walls where you can sleep using just your sleeping bag and pad. Mice are a frequent problem in these permanent fixtures, so many people staying in the shelters choose to set their tents up around them rather than actually staying in them. Most of the shelters are reserved for groups, so, unless you are part of a group or are lucky enough to be assigned to them, they are a part of the Wonderland Trail that you will not experience. A few of the camps also offer a similar, all-wood version of these shelters as a campsite. We had the potential to stay in one at South Mowich River, but it was already occupied by the time we arrived in camp.

The Wonderland Trail passes through Longmire Village at the southern end of the park. This provides an easy opportunity to spoil yourself with a night off-the-trail at the rustic, 25-room *National Park Inn*. Or you could opt for the historic, 121-room *Paradise Inn* at Paradise to enjoy comfortable lodging along with scenic dining. If the lure of a cozy bed and a hot shower sounds too good to pass up, be sure to make reservations for a room well in advance, particularly if hiking the trail in July or August.

ⓘ For more information on both lodges call Mount Rainier Guest Services at +1 (360) 569-2275 or reserve a room online at *http://www.mtrainierguestservices.com/*

It is also possible to camp in Mount Rainier's four frontcountry camp-grounds: *Cougar Rock, Ohanapecosh, White River*, and *Mowich Lake*. Making advance reservations or arriving early in the morning is necessary for camping within the park, particularly on summer weekends.

(i) For more information on frontcountry campgrounds refer to the National Park Service website or go to *http://www.recreation.gov/* to make a reservation.

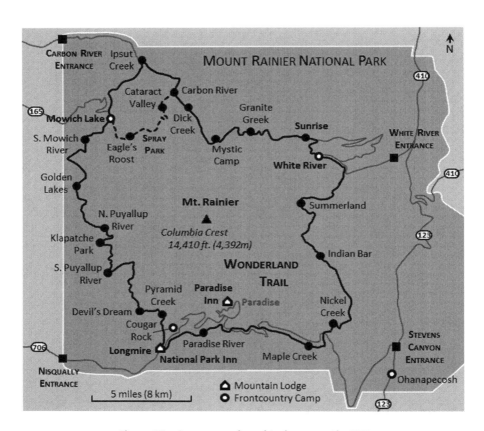

Figure 13 – Campgrounds and Lodges near the WT

5. Planning & Preparation

"Proper prior planning prevents pitifully poor performance." This is an old military adage that I picked up as a young Boy Scout that has stuck with me over the years and proven its worth. The message is clear – the more time you spend planning in advance of your trip, the less likely you are to forget something or overestimate your abilities, and the more likely you are to create a memorable and rewarding experience. This chapter is designed to take you through the thought process from big picture items, like when to hike the WT and how long to spend on the trail, to smaller, but important considerations, like what type of gear is appropriate and how much food to bring. With the proper forethought, you can do your best to eliminate variables and ensure maximum enjoyment on the trail.

a. Itinerary

In general, the itinerary planning process can be broken down into two stages. The first stage includes all activities concerning long lead items, such as permits and travel arrangements. The resulting 'macro-plan' is the organizational frame of the hiking trip. The second stage focuses on determining the specifics of your thru-hike, such as daily distances and desired campsites. The resulting 'micro-plan' is your personal hiking itinerary. In the case of the WT, there is an overlap between the two stages, since a detailed hiking itinerary must already be included as part of the advance permit reservation request.

Macro-Planning

Below is a simple flowchart that outlines the major steps you will take as you begin to plan your Wonderland Trail experience.

Figure 14 – Flow Chart Macro Planning

The most important part of planning your time on the Wonderland Trail is securing a permit. This is a time-sensitive issue as you must apply for the permit between March 15 and March 31. This process is described in detail in Section 4a *Permits & Regulations*. In order to apply for the permit, you must decide how long you plan to take to hike the WT based on your fitness and experience and how much time you have to escape into nature. Plan your route carefully, allowing some flexibility with start dates, direction, and choice of camps. Section 'Micro-Planning' below provides additional guidance on detailed route planning.

After submitting your permit application, you may not hear back from the park service before May 1, and it is possible that your request may not be fulfilled in the lottery after all. Regardless of any outcome, you may have to make travel arrangements before you have a permit, especially if you are flying into Washington rather than driving. If you later receive a denial letter, don't be discouraged. You may be able to secure a permit on a first-come, first-served walk-up basis. However, even with this option it is wise to have a plan B and plan C in case it doesn't work out. The good news is that there is plenty of great hiking in Mount Rainier National Park and in the surrounding area if you are willing to risk going there but discover that a permit for the entire trail is not possible. You may still be able to hike sections of the WT, like the 34-mile long Northern Loop or the 36-mile Eastern Loop, as an alternative. The National Park Service website offers a wide variety of alternative trails well worth exploring.

Micro-Planning

The goal of this planning stage is to map out your personal hiking itinerary. The first task is to confirm your initial ETD from Section 2b *Time*. Based on your final ETD, you will be able to derive your average daily mileage which serves as the basis for all subsequent itinerary decisions. Our advice is to choose an ETD that not only matches your fitness and ability but also allows you to enjoy the beauty of the WT and the grandeur of the mountain you are hiking around. The most important thing is to know yourself as a hiker. Consider your experience of multi-day backpacking trips, your relative level of fitness, and your deep motivations. Why are you hiking the WT and what do you hope to get out of the experience? Plan accordingly to maximize enjoyment and a successful completion of your trek.

For example, let's assume you conclude that spending 10 days on the trail is a reasonable estimate. This translates to 9.3 miles per day on average (93 miles / 10 days). The 9.3 miles/day estimate you can now use as the basis for determining the actual distances targeted for each individual day. Actual daily distances may need to be adjusted based on the difficulty of the trail section ahead and the preferred campsite location. If you are intending to resupply food at some point during your trip, the necessary stops or detours need to be incorporated in your itinerary as well.

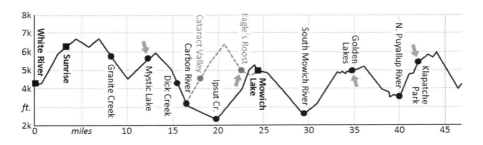

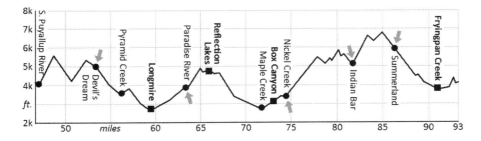

Figure 15 – Sample 10-day Itinerary

When you look at the elevation profiles in Figure 15 above and plan your route from one campsite to the next, you will find that a typical day's hike could take you up and down as much as 3000 feet. In other words, a vertical mile of gain and loss is common in a single day. For example, hiking from Mowich Lake Campground to Golden Lakes on the park's western side, a horizontal distance of only 10.3 miles, actually involves descending 2,324 feet followed by a 2,525-foot ascent. Your fitness and preparation for the WT will vary, but acknowledging the pie-crust-like profile of the circuit from the very beginning is important to making an informed decision about how far you will be able to hike each day.

To further assist you in creating your personal Wonderland Trail route, we have included sample itineraries in Appendix D, which provide options for both hiking directions (clockwise/counterclockwise) in combination with three different hiking speeds (leisurely/moderate/energetic).

b. Food

It is important to have all the food you intend to eat along the Wonderland Trail purchased, portioned, packed, and ready to take with you before arriving in Mount Rainier National Park to start your trek. Although there is a small park shop at Longmire with basic groceries available for purchase, it would be difficult to find everything you need for a successful backpacking trip there. Gateway towns just outside of the park entrances (Enumclaw, Buckley, and Ashford) offer rather limited supplies, so it is a better idea to shop at larger grocery and camping stores in Portland, Seattle, or Tacoma before heading to the park if you are flying in.

Food should not be underestimated in its ability to revive energy and keep spirits up. Looking forward to a good meal on the trail is motivational and having a satisfied stomach lets you fall asleep more contentedly at night. Putting effort into planning and preparing balanced meals with a lot of variety is well worth it. There's nothing worse than eating a meal that brings you little enjoyment. Refer to Appendix G for a comprehensive list of food suggestions.

Below are some guidelines for choosing the right kind of food when planning your trail menu:

- Nutritional value: choose high energy foods and ensure an adequate supply of vitamins and minerals

- Calorie distribution: balance approx. 15% protein, 60% carbohydrates, and 25% fat per meal
- Non-perishable: your food must not spoil for a week or longer at up to 90°F (30°C)
- Weight: your food should be as dry and light as possible (including packaging)
- Ease of preparation: save gas, time, dirty pots, and nerves after a long day of hiking

Two factors are particularly important to consider when determining how much food to bring on your journey – calorie value and pack space. Your meals should provide approximately 1.5-2 times the calories you usually consume per day. Calculate higher calories when in low temperatures and vice versa. Additional hunger can be satisfied with snacks. As on any multi-day backpacking trip, pack space is always at a premium. Make sure all food items have a dense nutritional value and are worth their weight and space. The less space you have, the less water and air content should be in your food packaging.

 As a rule of thumb, you should aim for about 1-2 pounds (½-1kg) of food per person per day.

In order to avoid space issues, it helps to repackage your food into single servings, let out any air, and cut off excess packaging. Zip lock bags work well as they can be labeled and reused for packing out waste. As you pack your food in your dry bags, try to make layers of meals per day rather than packing all breakfasts at the bottom, and so forth. This makes accessing your food more convenient. Furthermore, pack the most perishable food items at the top of your bag for early consumption.

In addition to your main meals, well-chosen snacks and supplements can provide valuable nourishment as well. As temperatures rise, it is vital to replenish electrolytes, such as sodium, chloride, potassium, magnesium, manganese, and calcium, on a consistent basis. High water intake without electrolyte replacement over many hours can lead to *hyponatremia*, a life-threatening condition where your body does not have enough salts to function. Adding salty snacks (pretzels, goldfish, salted nuts, or chips) and/or supplements to your trail diet helps avoid electrolyte imbalance.

> **!** If you are on a low sodium diet, ask your doctor if a higher sodium intake while on the trail would be appropriate for you.

As you plan your meals, mind the respective cooking times and utensils needed for preparation. Anything that requires boiling for over 10 minutes can be bothersome and can consume too much fuel. Similarly, excessive in-camp preparations, such as cutting, peeling, and mashing, or meals that require a lot of attention can be a hassle when exhausted or overly hungry. Many hikers plan their meals so that the only cooking gear required is a small gas stove, one pot, and one spoon. Nevertheless, whatever meals you decide to go with, bring along adequate equipment and know your tolerance for cooking and cleaning dishes in the backcountry. Of the many things to enjoy on this experience, consider whether you want cooking to be one of them. Will it be relaxing or feel like a chore? Plan your meals accordingly.

> **i** A good tip for the morning is to eat a quick cereal bar for breakfast, warm up while packing up, and get going faster to save time and gas needed for a hot breakfast later.

You may decide to alternate your food strategy depending on the campsite you are staying at, the arrival time, and the difficulty of the day ahead. For example, scenic spots and shorter trail days may invite you to enjoy a relaxing morning coffee or spend a long evening with celebratory dining. In summary, your food strategy is a matter of your personal preference, the tightness of your schedule, access to food and gas, and your resupply strategy.

c. Resupply

Depending on how long you plan to backpack the Wonderland Trail and how much weight you are able/willing to carry, you may need to resupply at some point during your adventure. The only opportunity for buying groceries along the trail is at the General Store at Longmire, which offers a limited supply of basic goods. A much more practical approach is to take advantage of the opportunity to cache food.

There are four convenient cache stations along the Wonderland Trail: *Longmire Wilderness Information Center, White River Campground, Sunrise Visitor Center*, and *Mowich Lake Patrol Cabin*. This means that no matter how long you decide to take to hike the trail, you can get away with carrying only a small portion of the food/fuel you will need at a time. On a 93-mile hike, the ability to reduce your pack weight is an amazing convenience. During our twelve days, we never had to carry more than a 4-day supply of food at a time, saving us enormous amounts of weight and space in our packs, and ultimately making the trip much more enjoyable.

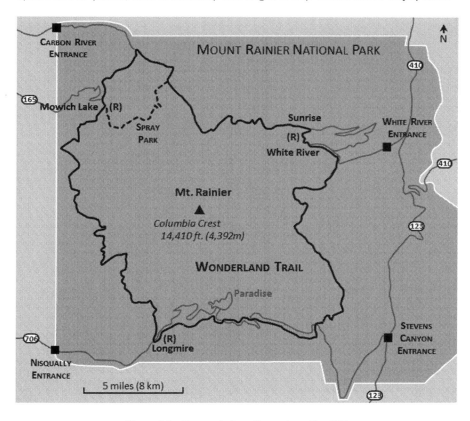

Figure 16 – Resupply Locations along the WT

Longmire Wilderness Information Center

This is a manned cache station, so be sure to time your arrival for opening hours. Call ahead to confirm arrival of your cache and to check with the staff about current hours of operation for pick up. Caches are stored inside the Longmire WIC from Memorial Day weekend to September 30. Outside of those times, contact a ranger at the Longmire Museum to drop off or pick up a cache.

Phone: +1 (360) 569-6650 (Memorial Day weekend to September 30); +1 (360) 569-6575 (all other times)

White River Campground or Sunrise Ranger Station

You must indicate on your container if you will be picking up the food cache at the White River Campground or Sunrise Ranger Station. Rangers hand deliver caches to White River or Sunrise from the White River WIC, so allow extra time for its arrival. Call ahead to confirm arrival of your cache and to check with the staff about current hours of operation for pick up. The Sunrise Ranger Station has a short season due to snow. Early and late hikers should use White River Campground.

Phone: +1 (360) 663-2425 (Sunrise); +1 (360) 569-6670 (White River)

Mowich Lake

Food caches are stored in a bear box outside of the Mowich Lake Patrol Cabin which is located along the trail around the lake. Rangers deliver caches to Mowich Lake from the Carbon River Ranger Station by hand, so send your package early and call to confirm its arrival. The Mowich Lake Road can be subject to early closure due to weather conditions.

Phone: +1 (360) 829-9639 (Carbon River Ranch Ranger Station)

Appendix H provides additional information about these cache locations, including shipping addresses and available carrier options.

Preparing Food Caches

Caching is easy. You simply pack your food and whatever else you would like to cache – clean socks, wet wipes, batteries, etc. – into a hard-sided, rodent-proof container (5-gallon plastic buckets, available at well-stocked hardware or home improvement stores, work great) and label it clearly with the following information:

- Food Cache For: (hiking party leader's name)
- Permit Number: (given on accepted reservation OR write "Walk-up Permit")
- For Pickup At: (name of cache station)
- For Pickup On: (exact date for advance permit OR date range of intended pick-up for walk-up permit)

Mailing Food Caches

Be sure to allow for plenty of time for your cache bucket to arrive by mail. We were out of the country for 6 weeks prior to starting the Wonderland Trail, so we mailed our cache long before our arrival. The park service recommends a minimum of *two weeks* in advance of your start date. You must mail a separate cache to each of the locations you intend to use as park staff will not transport your food caches around the park for you.

Figure 17 – Properly Labeled Bucket and Retrieving Food Cache at Mowich Lake

If you do not have a permit and are taking your chances on getting a walk-up permit, you can still mail your caches ahead of time. Instead of a permit number, write "Walk-up Permit" on your bucket and the date range you expect to pick up your cache. After finalizing your walk-up permit, you may realize that the date range was incorrect. Ask the park ranger to contact the ranger on duty at the cache station and alter the date on your bucket to match the new date. This is very important, as not all of the cache pickup points have a ranger on duty when you arrive to help look for any missing buckets.

[!] Remember that you cannot mail fuel as it is flammable. However, by late in the season, there is usually an excess of white gas (and some canisters) at the cache stations. Park staff is happy to donate any fuel that they have available to Wonderland hikers.

Dropping off Food Caches

It is also possible to drive your food and fuel to each of the cache locations, but you will need to allow a full day to do this, as the roads are not direct and the distances between each location significant.

We did a combination of mailing and dropping off caches. Because Mowich Lake is the most difficult cache location to reach by car, we decided to mail one of our caches there. Hoping to start hiking at White River, we entered the park at the Nisqually Entrance in the southwest corner and headed right to Longmire, where we applied for our permit. Permit secured, we left another 4-day cache of food and fuel there and then drove to our starting point at White River with our first 4-day supply of food and an 8-day supply of fuel. Before leaving, we asked the ranger at Longmire to contact the ranger at Mowich Lake to make sure that our cache shipment had in fact arrived by mail.

[i] Picking up your food cache is an exciting milestone on the trail. Be sure to pack yourself some special treats that you can enjoy. A box of wine, a can of potato chips, or any other little indulgence can go a long way to elevating your spirit in the backcountry.

Food Exchange & Caching Tips

There is also a food exchange bin at each cache station that allows backpackers the opportunity to leave extra food, take donated food, or exchange items. We ran into a mother-daughter pair on the trail whose mailed cache was not in the storage container at Mowich Lake when they arrived. Unfortunately, no park ranger was on duty at the patrol cabin that evening to help sort out the problem. They were able to gather enough food from the exchange box to keep them going on the trail. Many hikers, including us, donated extra food we were carrying to them after hearing of their predicament!

If you know you will be returning to a cache station after your Wonderland experience, it is also possible to leave your cache bucket with items you no longer want to carry on the trail and pick it up later. When we arrived at Longmire, we repacked our cache bucket with dirty clothes, spent camera batteries, and other items that we had discovered we were not really using during our first eight days on the trail, like hand sanitizer, microspikes, extra toilet paper, etc. After returning to our car at White River, we drove back to Longmire to pick everything up again. If we had known we could do this before starting out on the WT, we would have left some battery chargers for our cameras in the cache we dropped off at Longmire. This would have allowed us to charge our batteries in the Park Inn restaurant while eating our breakfast and then put the chargers back into our cache bucket until the end of our trip.

Special Treats

The Wonderland Trail passes through Longmire Village at the southern end of the park. This provides an easy opportunity to eat at the national park restaurant and buy simple groceries at the General Store. The restaurant is open all day and serves breakfast, lunch, and dinner, so plan your stop to coincide with your favorite meal. We couldn't wait for the opportunity to ditch our standard oatmeal breakfast and have some fresh eggs and biscuits, and they did not disappoint. We also picked up some cheese and cold beers at the park shop. Enjoying these treats with our lunch that day made us feel like we had died and gone to heaven! Many Wonderland hikers also make a 0.5-mile detour to visit the snack bar at Sunrise in the northeast corner of the park. The menu is limited, but the opportunity for cheeseburgers, hot dogs, French fries, and soft-serve ice cream proves to be a draw that many cannot resist.

d. Training

Whether the Wonderland Trail is your first or your fiftieth major multi-day backpacking trip, getting in shape for the physical and mental challenge of this epic adventure is essential to both your safety and your enjoyment on the trail. Your body must be prepared to hike 93 miles over 22,000 feet of elevation gain/loss. Your mind must be prepared to hike from 5-14 consecutive days, depending on the route you choose and how aggressive you want to be with your itinerary. You must also build the stamina to carry a backpack of 30-40+ pounds up arduous switchbacks and down glaciated valleys relentlessly. Knowing yourself as a hiker and what your body is capable of will improve your chances of successfully and gratifyingly completing the Wonderland Trail.

Mental Preparation

Hiking long distances over challenging terrain for days on end requires as much mental preparation as physical preparation. Being clear about your goals and aspirations for trekking the WT will help you be realistic about what you can accomplish physically and will remind you in the difficult moments why you chose to take on this challenge in the first place. The rewards of hiking the WT are many, from solitude in the forests to magnificent vistas on high ridges, but you would not want to miss these moments by not being prepared. Maintaining a positive attitude begins with training in advance and recognizing that there is value in developing routine, building mental and physical stamina, and pushing past initial pain and discomfort in order to build strength and confidence. Researching the Wonderland Trail, learning about its natural and human history, and reading about others' experiences on the trail via guidebooks, blogs, and websites can all help increase your investment in the adventure ahead. The more you do to prepare in advance, the better your enjoyment on the trail.

Physical Preparation

You will need endurance and strength to complete the demanding 93-mile loop. The hikers we encountered on the WT who were enjoying it most were the ones who had prepared and practiced in advance. They were the ones who had planned well and were taking time to "smell the roses", stopping to photograph "The Mountain", relaxing among the wildflowers as they took a snack break, or enjoying a peaceful moment near a waterfall with the pack off their shoulders. You certainly don't want to be the "rookie" on the trail who is easily recognized. These folks are usually carrying too much weight, are out of shape, complaining of blisters, and spending so much time worrying about themselves that they miss the beauty all around them. You are also more likely to injure yourself if you are not physically prepared. A sprained ankle or knee can limit or perhaps prematurely end your WT experience. You can prevent all of this by training well in advance for this rewarding but demanding physical challenge. Here are a few tips on how to do just that:

Practice Hiking

Develop a schedule and go hiking frequently. Wear the boots or shoes you intend to hike in, both to break them in if they are new and to ensure that they will be comfortable over long distances and not cause painful blisters. Begin with shorter distances of 1-3 miles and gradually add to that until you build up to distances that approximate your longest planned days on the WT. Keep in mind that a 7-day circuit could mean days as long as 15-18 miles. Even for a 10-12 day circuit, you will have long days of 12 miles or more. It is important, therefore, to construct a training regimen that develops your walking stamina to be able to walk for hours and miles a day.

Practice Hiking with a Backpack

Begin simply by hiking with your backpack (ideally the one you will carry on the WT) with no additional weight. Gradually add weight throughout your training regimen, building up eventually to a fully-loaded pack that includes all of your gear, water, and food up to the maximum weight you would carry after resupply. This will give you an opportunity to build stamina, get accustomed to how the pack sits on your waist and shoulders, and make adjustments in the straps for the best possible fit. You may also want to practice packing to make sure weight is distributed evenly (left to right and top to bottom) as an imbalanced pack can cause muscle and back soreness that only becomes evident after hiking for miles. Section 6b *Hiking* offers helpful tips on how to properly pack a backpack.

Practice Hiking in varied Terrain

Locate places to hike that will give you practice hiking on varied terrain, changing elevations so that you gain experience carrying the pack uphill and downhill and on uneven terrain. If you live near mountains and rolling hills, this will be a lot easier than if you live in pancake-flat Illinois as we do. One option, however monotonous, is to locate a place like a toboggan run with steps built next to it that will allow you to walk "uphill" and "downhill" continuously for a decent stretch. Even walking stairs in a multi-story building can help simulate the continuous climbing that you will inevitably experience on certain sections of the WT.

When we hike with a backpack, we generally plan to hike for an hour without stopping to take the packs off before giving ourselves a short 5-10 minute break for water and a small snack. It is important, once again, to know yourself as a hiker. As you are training, try to gain a sense of what your average distance per hour hiking is with a fully loaded pack. Knowing how many miles you can cover comfortably in an hour will also help you plan your days on the WT and let you know how early you will have to get on the trail each day to arrive in camp at your desired time.

Training Regimen

Begin training at least three months in advance. Be consistent. Set a schedule and stick to it. Your training regimen will necessarily vary based on your age, overall health, and current level of fitness. A good training regimen will incorporate aerobic exercise that will help control your cardiovascular rate for sustained periods of time as well as anaerobic strength-building exercises to help tone certain muscle groups. Vary your fitness training to include activities like biking, yoga, pilates, swimming, fitness classes, and lifting weights. It may be a good idea to consult a trainer to help you develop a training regimen that best fits your needs and your lifestyle. Finally, eat healthy and begin to research foods that are high in energy and low in weight. Try them out on your practice hikes so you know before you go which ones appeal to you and provide the energy you need to sustain long days on the trail.

For example, exercises with light to medium weights are great to strengthen shoulder and back muscles that will be needed for pole use. A good exercise can be done with dumbbells of 5-25 pounds (2-12kg), called "90 degree dumbbell lateral raise".

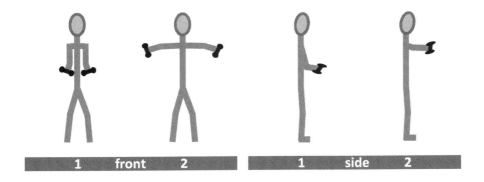

Figure 18 – Shoulder Exercise for Trekking Pole Use

Stand with your feet at shoulders' width, your back slightly slanted forward and your core muscles engaged. Start by holding the weights in your hands with your elbows in a 90° angle touching your ribs and under arms extended straight in front of your body. In a slow, smooth motion, raise elbows from your ribs to shoulders' height. Hold briefly and return into the starting position. Choose a weight that allows you to repeat at least 3 sets of 15-20 repetitions. Remember to engage both your abdominal as well as your lower back muscles to support a sturdy stance.

Hiking Style

In order for you to use your energy efficiently and keep strains to your joints and tendons at a minimum, it is useful to adopt a good hiking style. Pay particular attention to the following three things on the trail:

Hike at a sustainable pace

The Wonderland Trail is a rollercoaster circuit of Mount Rainier. There is relatively little flat hiking, so maintaining pace really means controlling your heart rate. Avoid hiking so fast that you are forced to take frequent breaks just to catch your breath. Instead, adjust your pace so that you can hike continuously for approximately an hour or longer without needing to stop in order to recover your energy. Good pacing is essential to tackling the repeated long ascents and descents that characterize the WT. Ultimately, a slow but sustainable pace will be the fastest way, because you feel less fatigue and need less rest/recovery time.

 Sing quietly to yourself, count, or chant a mantra that helps you regulate your breath and your pace.

Furthermore, hiking at a sustainable pace helps to keep your metabolism and energy conversion in an aerobic state. In brief, aerobic metabolism means that your muscles are receiving enough oxygen from your lungs, sufficient fuel through your bloodstream, and have enough time to dispose of by-products from burning the fuel, especially lactic acid.

The aerobic state or respiration is usually the sweet spot for your body to process its energy, from a nutritional intake as well as fat storage perspective. Keep in mind that even very fit people have an average body fat level of 5-15 percent. That means that a 160-pound person would have around 16 pounds of fat which contain approx. 56,000 calories – enough caloric energy for over 20 days. This body fat is a valuable reserve you should tap on the trail in order to keep your packed food weight low and potentially reduce your body weight as a pleasant side effect. Maintaining a sustainable pace allows you to do just that.

Take small steps

In line with maintaining a sustainable pace, small steps avoid stress peaks for your muscles, reduce the force of impact on your joints, and minimize the likelihood of an injury due to misstep. Although the Wonderland Trail is generally well groomed and fairly wide, the terrain does vary from time to time. Pay attention to rocks, roots, and other obstacles that could trip you up or cause you to twist an ankle.

Taking small, conscious steps keeps the strain on your muscles at a low level, avoiding muscle ache. Especially when hiking uphill with a full pack, small steps will reduce exhaustion and extend your range. Likewise, descending with a full pack causes many to suffer from knee and ankle pain. The larger the step, the greater the vertical drop there is and, hence, the greater the impact to your joints. Lastly, small steps are less likely to go wrong. A small step has less momentum that could potentially cause you to twist your ankle or slip on loose gravel. Since emergency access to the WT is limited, avoiding any injury is the best way to go.

Always place your feet in the direction of the slope of the trail

The last recommendation is especially important when hiking downhill. Look at the direction and angle of the slope. Always place your foot so that it is in line with the direction of the slope of the trail. If the path is going straight down the mountain, your toes should also point straight down. If there are switchbacks, you should adhere to the respective slope of the trail.

Why? Think of it this way: If you do slip, you want your toes to shoot up/forward. You may land on your bottom or your backpack – but both are usually padded. If you had your foot at an angle to the slope and slipped, your body weight would follow the slope and push forward, twisting your ankle and potentially causing a painful injury at an inconvenient location. So remember, always point your toes to the slope.

Trekking Poles

Trekking poles offer some definite advantages on a multi-day backpacking trip. They may extend your daily distance by up to 25%, because they increase the efficiency of each step and help conserve energy. They also keep your hands up and help with circulation in the arms, preventing your fingers from swelling. When carrying a heavy pack, especially one in which the weight is not evenly distributed, you can easily lose your balance. Using trekking poles guarantees three points of contact on the ground at all times and, thus, increases your stability.

On the WT, you will also cross several rivers and streams, some on narrow logs, others on stepping-stones. Your poles are especially handy here when a misstep can leave you with wet feet or worse! You may even have to ford a river if the bridge is out, so you will certainly want trekking poles to maintain your stability, especially when you cannot see where you are stepping. When descending, trekking poles can be used to slow down your forward movement and take the stress off of your knees. However, make sure to not overly strain your shoulders while relieving your knees.

(i) Make sure your poles are adjusted to a comfortable height, so that on a flat surface you are neither leaning too far forward or have your elbows bent at over 90 degrees. If you know you will be descending a steep section of trail for a prolonged period, you may want to lengthen the poles to prevent you from leaning too far forward. Conversely, you may wish to shorten the poles on prolonged steep uphill sections to help with the climb.

The propulsion aspect of the trekking poles is also important. Although your legs will undoubtedly be doing most of the work, your upper body can support them. Make sure that your poles are adjusted to the right length (approx. 0.7 x your height) and that the locking mechanism is securely latched.

Then, when taking a stride with the left leg, set your right pole in front of your right, rear foot (Figure 19, step 3). In this position, smoothly but forcefully push back. Then, gently lift the right pole tip slightly above the ground as you bring the left pole forward. Place the left pole in front of your left, rear foot (Figure 19, step 5). Engage and repeat.

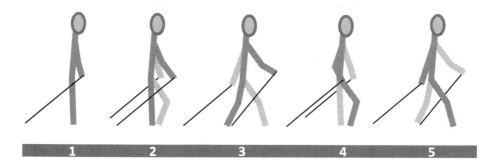

Figure 19 – Trekking Poles Use

Be sure not to ram the poles into the ground. This causes stress on your wrists and shoulders and leads to earlier exhaustion. Also, you don't want your energy to go straight into the ground, but rather into a forward movement. Note how in Figure 19 the poles are never vertical, but always at an angle so that you push forward and not down.

(!) Make sure to familiarize yourself with the right technique before heading out on the WT. When used incorrectly, trekking poles can cause pain and injuries to shoulders and wrists.

Allow yourself phases of rest from using your trekking poles. Hold them in their balanced middle while hiking along flat, easy stretches of the WT, with your shoulders either dangling down loosely or keeping your natural walking stride motion without the poles striking the ground.

(i) Before taking poles on any long-distance hike, it is very helpful to try them out to see how they feel. Practice the motion which is a little different from your usual one. If you cannot get comfortable or find that using the poles causes additional exhaustion, leave it at that. Especially, if you already have problems with your shoulders or wrists, poles may cause unnecessary stress.

6. Gear

Choosing the right gear to take on a multi-day backpacking trip is an essential component to creating a memorable and pleasant experience. For us, deciding on the right equipment is both exciting and nerve-racking.

Every year, companies make improvements in gear that make it lighter, stronger, more durable, and more functional, but the cost of all this equipment can add up in a hurry. So be patient, do  your research, choose wisely, and do not rush to replace your entire kit. We make it a habit to upgrade one or two items in our gear list each year. This section will help you consider the essential items for backpacking the WT and offer guidance on how to choose what is best for you.

a. Clothing

With a 14,000+ foot peak dominating its landscape, the weather in Mount Rainier National Park is controlled by "The Mountain" and can be highly unpredictable from day to day. While summer temperatures are often pleasant, it is important to be prepared for all types of weather while out there, from extreme heat to heavy rains to freak snowstorms. Additionally, you will often change thousands of feet in elevation and travel through a variety of terrain throughout the day, including dense old-growth forests, exposed subalpine meadows, and permanent snowfields. At night, your camps will range in elevation from 2,360 to 6,245 feet. While temperatures may climb during daylight hours, they can also cool off considerably once the sun goes down. How does one prepare for such a range of conditions? The answer is layers.

Layering

Layering your clothing is key to maintaining a comfortable temperature during your Wonderland Trail experience. You will likely wake up to chilly temperatures averaging in the mid-40s in the morning, and, as you break camp and get ready to hit the trail, you will want to dress warmly to be comfortable. While hiking during the day, your body temperature will rise quickly, and you will need to shed these warm layers to avoid overheating even though average high temperatures in summer months typically only reach a pleasant 65-75°F. During rest breaks and on exposed sections of the trail, you will cool down quickly and might need to throw on an extra layer to avoid cooling down too much. Upon arriving in camp, prepare for cooler evening temperatures by changing out of any wet or damp clothing and adding hats, gloves, warm jackets, and perhaps even long underwear as necessary.

Daytime

Typically, we slept each night in a pair of mid-weight long underwear and warm, dry camp socks. After waking up, we changed out of our bedtime apparel into our hiking gear for the day: hiking socks, zip-off pants, a wicking short-sleeved T-shirt, a warm long-sleeved layer over that, a down jacket, a warm hat, gloves, a neck gaiter, and sometimes even a rain jacket/windbreaker for extra warmth. We often shed the warm gear before leaving camp, making sure to keep everything accessible near the tops of our packs.

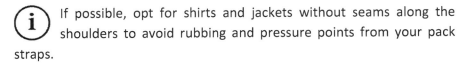 If possible, opt for shirts and jackets without seams along the shoulders to avoid rubbing and pressure points from your pack straps.

After a few hours on the trail, we normally zipped off our pant legs and layered down to short sleeves to deal with our rising body temperatures. Sunny skies and high elevations make sun exposure a serious consideration, so we also carried a lightweight, long-sleeved button-down shirt to cover our arms from the sun and to help keep mosquitos at bay, a baseball cap, and a multifunctional scarf for sun protection.

Nighttime

Upon arriving at camp and completing camp chores, we changed into our long underwear tops and down jackets (and windbreakers, hats, gloves, and neck gaiters as needed) to be dry and warm. We also really looked forward to giving our feet a break and getting out of our boots and into warm, dry socks and comfortable, lightweight camp shoes (synthetic clogs). At bedtime, we changed out of our hiking pants and into long underwear bottoms for sleeping.

One of your favorite items on the trail will be your camp shoes. Your feet will thank you for any time that you can find to be out of your hiking shoes. We always carry synthetic clogs with us. They are extremely lightweight and we enjoy being able to wear warm socks with them around camp at night. We can attach them to the outside of our packs if necessary when spare room is needed in our bags. They are also waterproof, making them additionally useful for having to make any wet water crossings.

Additional Tips

Hiking clothing has come a long way in recent years, and there are many stylish and comfortable options on the market. Whatever you choose to bring, it is important to remember that you will be carrying these items on your back for the length of your trip. Here are a few extra tips:

- Avoid over-packing and plan on wearing each item for several days at a time. We always need fewer changes of clothing than we think!
- Choose lightweight, wicking fabrics that dry easily when wet. Avoid cotton items like the plague and opt for shirts and pants made from synthetic materials instead.
- Make sure everything fits well, is comfortable, and won't stretch out after wearing it for days on end.

- Consider packing a lightweight belt to keep your pants up as you are likely to drop a few pounds on the trail.
- Long underwear made from merino wool will keep you cozy at night.

[!] Avoid polluting or contaminating natural water sources by using soap to wash your clothes. Consider carrying a collapsible bucket and keep at least a distance of 200 feet (60m) from any stream or lake.

Sample Clothing List

This was our clothing pack list (each):

3 pairs of hiking socks
1 pair of warm camp socks
3 sets of wicking underwear
2 sports bras (women)
1 long-sleeved underwear top
1 long underwear bottom
2 pairs zip-off hiking pants
3 short-sleeved T-shirts
2 long-sleeved T-shirts
1 long-sleeved button-down shirt

1 sun hat (wide-brimmed or cap)
1 multifunctional scarf/bandana
1 down jacket
1 rain jacket
1 rain pants
1 warm hat
1 gloves
1 warm neck gaiter
1 pair of camp shoes

b. Hiking

This section will offer advice and guidelines on a few of the essential items: footwear, backpacks, and trekking poles. These days, there are so many options available, and everyone has an opinion on what is best. It's a good idea to consult multiple sources before making decisions about key pieces of gear. We recommend reading up on product reviews in leading outdoor magazines, reading consumer reviews online, and consulting with experts at outdoor gear stores. In the end, the best gear is the gear that's right for you.

Shoes versus Boots

The single most important gear choice is deciding what to wear on your feet while hiking the Wonderland Trail. Nothing is worse than having sore feet, blisters, or a sprained ankle, and, since walking for 93 miles is what you've signed up for, it's important to consider a few basics.

Any good hiking shoe has a thick, cushioned sole with a non-slip tread. Beyond that, there are different opinions on which style is best suited for long-distance trekking – hiking boot, hiking shoe, or trail runner. The main differentiating factors are weight, stability, and protection from the elements.

Hiking Boot   Hiking Shoe   Trail Runner

Figure 20 – Hiking Shoes & Boots[2]

Hiking boots provide more stability to the ankles. A well-fitting boot is snug, supports the ankle, and reduces the risk of twisting on a slight misstep. With more contact area, the foot is less likely to move back and forth in a good boot. The high-rising sides also protect your ankles from rocks and roots and limit the amount of sand and dust entering the boot. Other advantages of a boot are warmth and water resistance. Drawbacks of boots are greater weight, stiffness (and hence resistance during walking strides), chances of blisters from ill-fitting boots, and lower breathability.

Boots vary greatly in stiffness of the sole, from a minimal shank to a ¾ shank to a full shank. This is important when considering the terrain you

---

[2] Sketches of Asolo boot and Salomon shoes.

will be hiking over. A full shank boot will bend very little when walking on uneven surfaces and boulder hopping, while a boot with a minimal shank will flex quite a bit. This can have a real effect on foot soreness at the end of a long day of hiking.

Hiking shoes combine the grip stability of a good boot with more flexibility. The low cut allows more mobility, while the light mesh uppers enable moisture wicking. Look for firm heel support and a hard, molded toe cap to protect your toes. Different brands have various lacing systems, some enable great fit in minimal time. Hiking shoes are lighter than boots and generally feel less restrictive while still providing sufficiently firm stability. Drawbacks are reduced ankle support and incompatibility with crampons (irrelevant for the WT in the summer).

Trail runners go one step further regarding agility and lightness, weighing about as much as a running shoe. In order to save that weight, trail runners usually provide less cushioning than hiking shoes, while still offering good tread and lots of grip. Upper materials are mostly breathable, light meshes that offer more support than running shoes but far less than a boot. Quick lacing systems are also available. Generally, trail runners are aimed at people going for a run in the mountains or woods, not necessarily long hiking trips with heavy backpacks. Drawbacks are low overall support and cushioning as well as minimal protection and water resistance.

Whichever shoe or boot you decide to go with, make sure you are confident about your choice. It should provide adequate support that is proportional to your body and your pack weight, wick moisture from your feet, not be too heavy and tiring, have a well-cushioned sole, and, most importantly, a padded inside that does not cause blisters. Get at least half a size bigger than you normally would so that you can wear padded socks (or a liner plus hiking sock) and to prevent your toes from hitting against the tips when descending. This will also allow for additional space as your feet will have a tendency to swell as you hike, especially on warmer days.

There is an old hiking adage that says, "A pound on your feet equals five pounds on your back." The idea is that weight carried on your feet is disproportionately more exhausting over long distances than weight carried on your back. For some hikers it may be worth it to choose lighter footwear if it helps you complete each segment of the WT more efficiently or with less wear and tear on your body.

> ⚠ We strongly recommend using your hiking shoes on a few hikes to break them in and see how they handle before heading out on the WT. If in doubt, try another pair – getting your shoes right is essential. Do not take shoes that are too worn down and have little tread left as this becomes a safety hazard.

Socks & Gaiters

A good sock can significantly add to your hiking comfort. Most modern trail socks are made of merino wool or polyester. Both fibers have outstanding properties regarding moisture wicking and temperature regulation. Thick socks, especially those with hidden seams, provide cushioning and help the shoe evenly embrace your foot, reducing rubbing and blisters. Though less stylish in a shoes-shorts combo and slightly warmer, socks that go (well) above your ankle collect less sand and stones, keep your legs cleaner, and protect against the sun.

Another way to keep out sand and stones (and snow if you encounter it) are gaiters. In addition to knee-high gaiters for snow treks, there are also short and light ones, specifically designed for hikers wearing shorts and low socks. The gaiters wrap around above your ankle and go over your shoes, protecting the gap between sock and shoe from unwanted entrants.

Compression socks can be of use especially to those who have issues with blood clots, edema, or thrombosis. Compression socks come in different lengths, from knee- and thigh-high, to full pantyhose style. There are different compression gradients to assist circulation. Lower gradients are usually prescription-free while higher gradients may require consultation. In either case, if you are aware of a condition or are over 40, it may be wise to get your doctor's opinion on using compression socks during your trek.

Backpacks

There is a multitude of backpack styles, capacities, and functionalities available in the market. Similar to other gear items, finding the right model depends on the nature of your trip and personal preference. In any event, it is important to find one that matches your personal physique. Given the extra weight you will be carrying, an ill-fitting backpack can cause considerable pain – chaffing along the straps and back aches from a too restrictive fit. Below is a list of decision criteria to help find a pack that is right for you:

Criteria	Comment		
Size	**Size**	**Torso [inch]**	**Torso [cm]**
	Extra Small	up to 15 ½	up to 40
	Small	15 ½ - 17½	40 - 45
	Medium	17½ - 19½	45 - 50
	Large	19½ and up	50 and up

Size (continued):

These are commonly used sizes. Learn how to measure your torso further below. Some packs also come in different hip sizes – measure at the widest part.

Apart from the torso size, the design and cut varies on packs and shoulder straps, making them more or less comfortable for broad- or narrow- shouldered people, etc. Compare and try different packs.

Capacity:

Typical packs used on the WT have capacities of 50-65 liters. All packing capacity is measured in liters based on a medium size pack. Small and large sizes can vary by +/- 3 liters.

While you want to choose the smallest capacity to save weight, you also need to fit all your gear. The right capacity for you depends on how bulky your big

	items are, e.g., your tent, sleeping bag, and sleeping pad, as well as how much and which clothing you plan to bring. Packs allow some flexibility by raising the top lid or strapping a tent or foam pad on the outside. However, this may mean that weights are not optimally distributed. See Section *'Pack & Adjust your Pack'* below for details.
Weight	As with most other gear, the weight of a backpack is closely linked to comfort and price. Thick, comfortable padding along shoulder straps and hip belts as well as the type of frame (internal, external, frameless) affect your base weight. However, keep in mind that you will be carrying this pack 5-10 hours per day for 5-14 days depending on your itinerary.
	The durability of materials affects the pack's weight. Light packs usually have very thin shell materials that require more caution with handling. They may also be less water-resistant than packs that are more rugged. This is a less crucial decision criterion, however, as you can attach a waterproof cover or use a lightweight pack liner in the event of rain.
Padding	The padding of shoulder straps, hip belt, and backside of the pack is the essential factor for how you perceive the comfort of a pack, especially when filled with up to 45 pounds (18kg) of gear and food. Ultra-light packs save weight, but make sure you are comfortable with the limited padding and that there is no rubbing/ chafing when the pack is fully loaded and you are in normal hiking motion.
Adjustability	Most modern internal frame packs are very similar regarding their adjustability. Shoulder straps and hip belts can be adjusted in length; load lifter straps

	connect the pack's top to the shoulder straps and keep the weight balanced near your center; sternum straps connect the shoulder straps across the chest to snug the pack's fit and increase stability. Some packs have an adjustable suspension, meaning the entire shoulder harness system can be slid up and down to customize the pack to the exact torso length. Compression straps along the sides and front of the pack pull the weight close to your center and keep contents from shifting on difficult trail sections. Adjustable straps and tool loops allow you to attach and adjust gear on the outside of the pack.
Compartments	Some bags divide the main compartment into two smaller zones. Separate compartments may not be a key decision factor, but they can help with organization, packing, and access to gear while on the trail. Some hikers may prefer to pack their sleeping bag in the lower compartment, keeping it separate from food and cooking gear. Side pockets can be useful for storing water bottles if you prefer this method to an internal hydration system. An outer mesh pocket can be handy for quick access to your rain gear and for storing it when wet. Often, the top flap provides storage for smaller items, such as sunglasses, sunscreen, lip balm, headlamp, hat, and gloves that you may want easy access to. Multiple compartments may conflict with a minimalist, ultra-light approach – just because you can carry it does not mean you should carry it.
Ventilation	A well-ventilated back area with airy padding is a big plus, especially on the WT, so keep this in mind when choosing a pack. It not only adds to your general

	comfort, but a dry back and shoulders are also less susceptible to chafing. Different brands and models have various approaches on how to wick moisture and heat from in between your back and your pack. Some have air channels between padding, others completely separate the pack from the hiker's back with a tension mesh. Some ventilation methods are more effective or comfortable than others. Try them out to find the one that works best for you.
Hydration	Space for an internally-mounted hydration reservoir is a standard feature on most packs along with a small opening for the drinking hose. This allows you to insert a reservoir with a capacity of up to three liters inside the pack, if that is your preferred hydration method.
Frame	There are two primary frame styles for multi-day backpacking trips: internal and external frames. Most modern packs employ internal frames sewed into the bag that conform to the shape of your back. Internal frame packs are more stable on uneven surfaces as they shift with your body better. Most packs are top-loading, but some offer a zippered front panel for easier access. Internal frame packs can be more expensive than external frames, but weight, comfort, and ease of use are more important factors. External frame packs, which used to be the norm, can be useful for carrying heavier loads and bulky items which can be attached to the outside. Although generally more affordable, external frame packs have limited adjustability, are less stable on uneven terrain, and are usually less water-resistant.

	Some ultra-light hikers choose frameless packs to shed even more weight, but this is generally not recommended for long-distance trekking.
Water Protection	Water protection for your backpack is essential to keeping your clothes and sleeping bag dry on the WT. One option for this is to carry an external rain cover. Some backpacks come with a built-in rain cover, or you can purchase one separately that fits the size of your pack. Either way, the rain cover should be easily accessible, allowing you to quickly protect your gear in the event of rain.
	Another popular option is to use an internal water-proof bag liner to pack all of your gear in. You can buy a lightweight, waterproof bag specifically made for this, or some budget-conscious hikers may choose to use heavy-duty trash bags or trash compactor bags. The advantage of using an internal liner is that your gear always has waterproof protection, eliminating the need to stop and put on a pack cover when it rains. The disadvantage is using a liner may make packing slightly more difficult and does not offer any water protection for gear stored in the external pockets of your pack.

Table 4 – Backpack Decision Criteria

We recommend using an internal frame pack with a maximum capacity of 70 liters, preferably smaller. On our 12-day Wonderland Trail experience, we carried our gear in heavy-duty nylon packs that weighed 4.5-5 pounds unloaded. We estimate that our fully loaded weight was approximately 40-45 pounds. For our upcoming backpacking trip, we have switched to lighter weight, internal frame packs that weigh less than 3 pounds unloaded. We are also converting to a lighter weight tent and sleeping bags in an effort to bring our base weight down below 20 pounds. For us, the most important features in a backpack are weight (unloaded), carrying capacity (enough room for gear, clothing, food, a camera, and a little spare room so that it is not completely stuffed), functionality (we prefer several smaller zip pockets and mesh pockets for storing smaller items), and adjustability (we prefer lots of straps to adjust the fit and properly center the load).

Excursion – Measuring your torso length:

1. Locate your 7th cervical vertebra (C7) at the base of your neck by tilting your head forward. It is the bony bump at the end your vertical spine as your neck is leaning forward. When you run your fingers down your neck, you will first feel the smaller C6 and then C7. This marks the top of your torso.
2. Locate your iliac crest at the top of your hip bone by placing your hands high on your hips. With your thumbs in the back, dig into your pelvis to find the rounded, highest point of your hip bone. The imaginary line between your thumbs marks the bottom of your torso.
3. Measure between top and bottom of your torso. Be sure to stand straight. Assistance while handling the tape measure is helpful.

Pack & Adjust your Pack

As you pack your backpack, pay attention to two important details: the weight distribution and the internal organization of your gear.

Regarding weight distribution, it is important to keep heavy items close to your back and centered, both vertically and horizontally (see Figure 21 below). Moderately heavy items should be placed around the heavy items, light ones along the perimeter of the pack (e.g., placing your sleeping bag in the bottom compartment, if your pack has divided compartments). The aim is to bring the weight in the backpack as close to the center of your back as possible. This way, the pack's center of gravity is closest to your own, making it less likely for you to lose your balance.

A well-considered internal organization and distribution of gear among the compartments and pockets of your pack can improve efficiency as you set up and take down your camp each day. Gear that will only be used in the evening can be placed inside and below heavy items. Tent poles can also be separated from the tent pack for better storability. Depending on the specific partitioning of your pack, you will see in the first days of hiking, which compartments are best suited for which gear. Try to develop a system of organization that you can repeat each day.

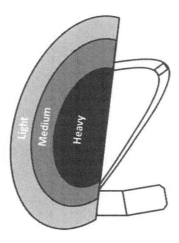

Figure 21 – Ideal Backpack Weight Distribution

For easier organization in the main compartment, it is good to use thin, waterproof bags or water-resistant compression sacks. They can be individually stuffed and make accessing contents more convenient while providing additional protection against water and dirt. Valuables (phone, keys, money) can be kept in a zip-lock bag and buried, as they will rarely be needed. Keep rain gear and waterproof pack cover (if used) easily accessible. Once you have all your items in place and are ready to take off, tighten all compression straps. They are usually located on the sides of your pack and at the top. Tightening the compression straps brings the weight closer to your back and prevents gear from shifting as you walk.

ⓘ Anything that needs easy and frequent access, such as a map, sunscreen, snacks, headlamp, or a pocket knife, should be stored in an accessible outside pocket near/on the top.

How to Adjust Your Pack

Adjusting your pack starts by putting it on correctly. If your pack is heavy, place one foot forward and lift the pack onto your thigh. Then, slip into the shoulder straps and lean forward, pulling the pack onto your back. As you lean forward, position the pack so the hip belt is centered comfortably over your hip bone, then close and tighten the hip belt firmly. As you straighten yourself up, your shoulder straps should be loose and 100% of the pack's weight should be on your hips. In this starting position, the shoulder straps should have a gap of approx. one inch over your shoulders (however, the anchor points of the shoulder harness will be below your shoulders). If the straps already put pressure on your shoulders in the starting position and your pack has an adjustable suspension, slide the entire shoulder harness up a little and re-secure it. Now, tighten your shoulder straps so they touch your shoulders.

Unlike traditional backpacks, today's packs are supported primarily by the hip belt with only approximately 10% of the weight being carried by your shoulders. Keep this in mind as you adjust and tighten the straps. Then, pull your load lifters (which extend from the top of your shoulder straps to the top of your pack) so that they form a 45-degree angle to a horizontal axis. This brings the pack's center of gravity closer to yours. Now, close your sternum strap and tighten comfortably in front of your chest. This reduces the pack's tendency of pulling your shoulders back. Finally, check your shoulder straps again. The shoulder straps should not be under great tension. Make sure you are merely guiding the weight and keeping it close to your center of gravity rather than carrying it with your shoulders.

Trekking Poles

Section 5d *Training* offered some advice on how to correctly use trekking poles. They can be of great service both for propulsion and providing balance as well as a sense of security on steep stretches of the trail. Below is some advice on what to look for when purchasing trekking poles:

- Good fit of grip and wrist strap: avoid sweaty grips (cork is good) and chafing straps.
- The length of the pole should be easily adjustable.
- The locking mechanism, as well as the overall pole, should be sturdy.
- Consider 1-, 2-, or 3-piece poles. Poles that collapse or fold are easier to store when not needed or when you want both hands free (e.g., when crossing a suspension bridge).
- The lighter the pole, the better. Lighter weight facilitates correct use and is less exhausting.
- Shock absorbers can be useful but are mostly a matter of taste. Try them out.
- Rubber tips absorb shock and muffle impact noise. They provide more grip on rock but less on soft subsoil. These tips can be removed when you need a sharper point for stability.

(i) If traveling by airplane, be aware that you are not allowed to bring trekking poles as carry-on baggage with you. Be sure to buy trekking poles that can fit inside your backpack or checked luggage. Another option is to attach trekking poles to the outside of your pack and then pack your entire kit inside a protective duffel or heavy-duty trash bags.

c. Sleeping

For most hikers on the WT, a lightweight tent is the preferred option for sleeping and shelter. Your tent is your home away from home, and a good night's sleep is the reward for reaching your destination after a long day on the trail. Although most hikers opt for a tent, sleeping bag, and a pad, there are alternatives for those looking to save weight and space in their packs.

Shelters

If you are hiking as a couple, you will probably share a tent and take advantage of the weight savings. Should you be joined by a hiking buddy, the weight savings may or may not be exceeded by the benefits of separate sleeping arrangements. It is probably a good idea to know in advance if your hiking buddy snores or shifts around a lot at night, so you can decide whether or not this is something you can tolerate. Earplugs are only effective to a certain point. Figure 22 below shows the four most common options to choose from when it comes to your sleeping shelter.

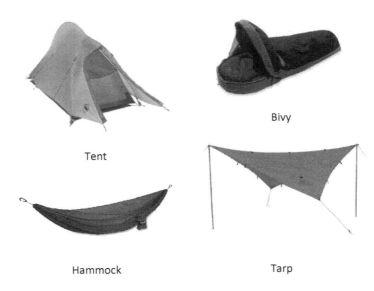

Tent

Bivy

Hammock

Tarp

Figure 22 – Sleeping Shelter Options[3]

Tent

A tent is the heaviest option, but it also provides the best protection from wind, water, and cold. It offers the most space for getting dressed and provides a space for journaling, reading, relaxing, or listening to music free of bugs. Most tents come with a vestibule that allows you to store your gear outside the tent and still protect it from rain. Some vestibules are configured in such a way that you could prepare food outside the tent but with some shelter from wind and rain. Tents come in 3- or 4-season models for use by 1-4 persons when backpacking. A 3-season tent is sufficient for use on the WT. The weight of backpacking tents continues to decrease with

---

[3] Tent: Big Agnes; Bivy: Outdoor Research; Hammock: ENO; Tarp: Kelty

improvements in technology. It is now possible to pack a 2-person tent that weighs less than 2 pounds. Most hikers add a footprint (a sheet of treated nylon placed under the tent) to protect against moisture and puncture to the tent floor. One disadvantage of a tent is that it has more surface area to collect moisture from rain and condensation, which will add weight to your pack if you do not have time to dry it out before packing and hitting the trail.

(i) Consider taking a small sponge to wipe dry any moist surface area before packing your tent. There are lightweight options made from viscose that have excellent absorption capabilities.

Hammock

In areas with ample trees of sufficient strength, hammocks are a great alternative to the 1-person ground systems described above. Their construction is independent from underground surfaces and slopes, so there is more flexibility in choosing campsites. When properly set up using wide tree-straps, hammock systems have a lower impact on vegetation versus pitching a tent or tarp on forest soil. Advocates state that hammocks are more comfortable than ground systems, however, individual perceptions may vary based on the preferred sleeping position. In combination with a rain fly, hammocks are a great solution in wet conditions, keeping you and your gear dry well above moist ground and puddles. On the downside, hammock campers are more sensitive to cooling from underneath, especially if there is wind, and, hence, additional insulation may be required (e.g., down under-quilt or foam padding). In areas with lots of bugs, a mosquito net may be another useful addition. Basic hammocks with no extras may help save pack weight, a complete hammock system, however, can weigh just as much if not more than a standard ground system.

Most of the campsites on the WT are wooded, making hammocks a viable option. Recall, however, that you must camp in established campsites. For the most part, trees will be located around the periphery of the cleared tent pad. It could be a challenge to find two suitable trees from which to string your hammock that are still within the bounds of the established site. Be careful not to crush vegetation if you find yourself getting creative. We did see a few hikers using hammock systems, and we were quite envious of the comfortable spot they had to relax in camp after a hard day's hike.

Bivy

A bivy (short for bivouac sack) is slightly bigger than a sleeping bag. It takes up less space in your pack than a tent and also weighs less. The sleeping bag slides into the bivy, which is made of water- and wind-resistant material. A bivy bag has a small hole or breathable fabric in the head area and is either left open or zipped shut. It also features a little dome in the head area, giving you some space to rest on your elbows inside. While bivies offer similar insulation and protection from the elements as tents, inner condensation is a greater problem, because the bivy gets in direct contact with the sleeping bag and has less air circulation. Bivies offer no additional space for gear or greater movement, and people who are uncomfortable in confined spaces may not enjoy the lack of freedom.

Under the Stars/Tarp

To anyone counting ounces, a tent, a hammock, or even a bivy may seem like unnecessary extra weight. The lightest alternative would be to sleep under the stars in your sleeping bag with the aid of a ground sheet and a tarp in case of rain. This option certainly helps save weight but lacks the wind protection and insulation of a tent or a bivy. Still, it offers a chance to experience nature up close and personal and to appreciate the night sky when it is clear. When choosing this alternative, make sure your sleeping bag is adequate to combat the temperatures including the wind-chill. A simple tarp is the lightest and cheapest shelter but offers the least protection and privacy.

On the Wonderland Trail, we used a 3-season, 2-person tent with a footprint as our shelter. Although we were incredibly fortunate not to experience any bad weather, we did enjoy the protection and warmth that our tent provided. We kept our boots, packs, and poles under the vestibules at night and enjoyed having adequate space to move around inside the tent. We also enjoyed being able to read books and write in our journals in the warmth of our tent as the temperature dropped in the evenings. Because we camped each night in relative close proximity to other campers in the established sites, it was nice to have our tent as a space where we could change clothes and clean up in privacy.

Sleeping Bags

Sleeping bags come in an overwhelming range of varieties based on their primary purpose. It is all the more important to understand which features are essential for a multi-day backpacking adventure on the Wonderland Trail. A sleeping bag is a significant investment that should last for 10+ years if cared for properly. There are three primary factors to consider: temperature rating, type of insulation, and weight.

Temperature Rating

Warmth, expressed by the bag's temperature rating, is your primary decision factor. Fortunately, there is a standardized warmth measurement – the European Norm (EN) 13537 – that helps you easily compare bags (see example in Figure 23 below). Ratings provide a measure of the bag's ability to keep you warm, ranging from its 'comfort' zone to the 'lower limit' and even to 'extreme'. The 'comfort' rating refers to lowest outside temperature at which a standard woman can sleep comfortably. The 'lower limit' refers to the lowest outside temperature at which the bag will keep a standard man warm. The 'extreme' rating refers to a survival-only scenario for a standard adult woman. In general, women need a slightly warmer bag to feel comfortable sleeping in cold weather.

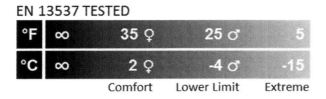

Figure 23 – Temperature Rating Example

Depending on which month you are planning to hike, choose a bag with a comfort rating that is equal to or lower than the average low temperature of that month. For example, average daily lows on the WT in July, August, and September (the only months you can hike the WT) drop to around 42°F (5.5°C), so your sleeping bag should have a comfort zone of 40°F (4°C) or lower to be on the safe side. A 3-season sleeping bag should be adequate to keep you warm at all elevations along the WT.

(i) For those who would like additional warmth, adding a sleeping bag liner is an option. They are made of silk, cotton, fleece, or synthetic materials and can add 5-15 degrees to your bag. In addition, sleeping bag liners keep your bag clean of dirt and body oils that can degrade its warmth over time.

Insulation

There are three types of insulation: down (goose or duck), water-repellent/treated down, and synthetic. Down is a natural, breathable material that provides incredible loft (air space for trapping the warmth of your body) and insulation for its light weight. It also compresses well, making it easier to fit in your backpack. However, if down gets wet, it tends to clump and lose its insulating power. There are new treated downs that either repel moisture or maintain insulation properties after getting wet. Many people prefer synthetic fill materials that mimic the great properties of down but are more water-resistant. Synthetic bags do not compress as well as down but are often more affordable. Look for sleeping bags with a fill power of 700-900, a rating of the bag's ability to loft and retain warmth.

Weight

Weight is a general concern. Besides the filling, the weight is a function of length, girth, cut, fabric, and features of the bag. Length of the bag is usually a pretty clear decision based on your height. Girth will primarily be determined by your shoulders and belly or hips. Cut refers to the bag's shape. Most backpacking bags available today are mummy style that follows the contours of the body – wider at the shoulders and narrow along legs and feet. Some bags are cut straight, providing more space but also more material to carry. Fabrics lining the sleeping bag are usually made of lightweight, synthetic materials. Features that enhance the bag's ability to retain heat include a drawstring hoodie to prevent heat loss from your head, a draft tube that covers the zipper to avoid heat loss on the side, and baffles or shingles that trap the down/synthetic fill in compartments to maintain even heat retention.

Combining the above aspects leads to the warmth-to-weight ratio. This figure compares the bag's temperature rating to its weight. Best ratios are achieved with hood-less, no-frills, down mummy bags that have reduced padding in the back. However, going ultra-light requires some experience, especially on how to substitute certain weight savings on one piece of gear with another gear item that is already part of your essentials. If it requires adding another piece of gear that is non-essential, it defeats the purpose. For instance, the lack of an attached hood on a sleeping bag can be compensated with a hooded down jacket and/or a warm hat, which anyone will most likely pack anyway. The padding in the back of a sleeping bag, which gets compressed when lying on it and, hence, loses its insulating properties, can be reduced if the sleeping pad offers sufficient insulation and when the hiker has a habit of lying flat on that side.

Lastly, choosing your sleeping bag must match your choice of camping strategy. If you decided to sleep without a shelter, your sleeping bag should be particularly warm, wind- and water-resistant. However, water-resistant shells are less breathable and require more time for your bag to loft. If you are planning to save weight on filling and frills by wearing your down jacket instead, make sure the sleeping bag provides enough inner space for the jacket's loft. In the end, deciding on one bag will be a compromise between all the contending traits and staying within a reasonable budget.

We used our 3-season goose down sleeping bags which are rated to +10°F (women's) and +15°F (men's) with a synthetic liner that added 5°F of warmth, and we were perfectly comfortable at night. As soon as we set up our tent, we opened the valves on our self-inflating sleeping pads, pulled our sleeping bags out of their stuff sacks and placed them in the tent to allow them to loft properly.

Sleeping Pads

A sleeping pad should literally support a good night's sleep. The two main criteria are cushioning and insulation. After a long day of trekking on the WT, you will appreciate some sort of sleeping pad. There are three popular and equally suitable alternatives – air pads, self-inflating pads, and foam pads – each with their own trade-offs.

Air Pads – Similar to the ones used in swimming pools, hiking air pads have a thin, air-tight shell that is inflated through a mouth valve. In order to cut down on weight, they are often semi-rectangular in shape. Air pads are very lightweight, can roll-up very small, and offer exceptional cushioning, especially those with a thickness of two inches (5cm) and up. On the downside, inflating a thick pad may require several minutes of lung power from you, which can feel like a chore at the end of the day. Lightweight models can be noisy due to crackling material. Punctures are also a concern, but this can be repaired in the field with the proper materials.

Foam Pads – Usually made of dense, closed-cell foams, foam pads can either be rolled up or folded like an accordion. They are light, inexpensive, provide great insulation, and are practically indestructible even on rough surfaces. When folded up, they also make convenient seats in camp. On the downside, foam pads are usually not very thick and provide limited cushioning comfort. They also do not compress and must therefore be attached to the exterior of your pack.

Self-inflating Foam Pads – Combining the packability of an air pad with the cushioning of a foam pad while needing only little additional inflation, thin pads are light and can be compressed well to fit into a small sack. On the downside, they offer limited cushioning, while thicker pads of over two inches are often too heavy for backpackers.

Whichever option you choose, make sure the pad is long enough and sufficiently wide at your shoulders. A good test is placing the pad on a hardwood floor or tiles and giving it a trial night of sleep.

After a long day of hiking and carrying heavy backpacks up and down thousands of feet of elevation each day, getting a good night's sleep is of utmost importance. Your body needs a proper rest and adequate time for recovery before getting up the following morning to do it all over again. Make sure you are comfortable sleeping on whichever pad you choose. We have recently changed from self-inflating foam pads to manually inflated air pads and feel that the savings of space and weight plus the added comfort is well worth the extra bit of effort required to blow up the pads.

Additional Comfort

Optional sleeping gear that can add to your comfort includes the clothing you wear in your sleeping bag, a pillow, an eye mask, and earplugs.

It's a wise idea to change into dry clothing once you reach camp and have your tent set up. At night you may want to wear long underwear and a light thermal top as an additional layer of warmth and to keep the inside of your sleeping bag free of dirt and body oils. Adding a dry pair of socks, hat, gloves, and fleece can help with heat retention and enjoying a good night of sleep. This is both a matter of personal choice and reflection of how cold it is at night.

A pillow can also add comfort, but it represents additional space and weight. Several models are available in different sizes, shapes, and materials. A good backpacking pillow will pack down to a very small size and weigh very little as this is a non-essential item.

An alternative to packing an inflatable pillow is using your sleeping bag's stuff sack as a casing and stuffing it loosely with clothes.

Eye masks can be helpful for those who are sensitive to light during a bright or full moon. Earplugs can be useful if noise prevents you from getting to sleep. Many backpackers, however, prefer to be alert to possible critters lurking around at night, which could include mice, skunk, porcupine, or even bear on the WT.

d. Food & Water

While Section 5b *Food* discussed the type of food and drinks to bring and send as resupply, this section focuses on the various gear items needed to store, prepare, and consume food as well as to treat and store water.

Food Storage

All the backcountry campsites along the Wonderland Trail are equipped with super convenient bear poles, so it is not necessary to carry your food in a bear canister. It is important to pack all of your food in a waterproof bag, as it will be hanging out in the elements overnight. There is a variety of lightweight, waterproof options available to choose from.

You are requested never to leave your food and scented items (toiletries, cooking utensils, sunscreen, bug repellant, etc.) unattended and to hang them overnight. Simply pack everything into a waterproof bag, remove the provided placement pole, hang your bag from the end of the placement pole, and then hoist your bag up to place it on one of the prongs at the top of the bear pole. Simply repeat the process in reverse to remove your belongings whenever you need them.

We loved not having to carry bear canisters while on the WT, but be aware that using the bear poles can be a little tricky. Hoisting a heavy bag filled with food, garbage, and toiletries on the end of a 10-foot pole and placing it onto another pole high in the air takes a lot of upper body strength, a very steady hand, and a good deal of patience. Whenever we hung or removed our bags, we always felt like we were participating in a physical challenge like you might see on the television show *Survivor*. Keep in mind that packing your food and scented items into several smaller bags may make the whole hanging process much easier.

Stove & Fuel

The preparation of your meals will undoubtedly require a stove, as campfires are prohibited on the Wonderland Trail. There are two basic stove-fuel systems most commonly used by backpackers: disposable gas canisters and refillable liquid fuel canisters.

Disposable Gas Canisters

Disposable gas canisters are filled with a pressurized gas mix of isobutane and propane. They have a self-sealing valve at the top and a thread. The thread can be used to mount a stove directly onto the top of the canister, using it as a stand. Gas canister stoves are extremely light (< 3oz/85g) and pack very small.

Stoves can also be connected to the gas canister via a fuel line. This way, the canister can be turned upside down (also referred to as "inverting"). This allows the canister to operate in liquid feed mode, which eliminates the need for the gas to vaporize inside the canister (which is necessary in case of the top-mounted option). By avoiding the need for vaporization, the gas can be used at lower (sub-evaporation) temperatures without losing performance. This is particularly useful in colder conditions. In addition, placing the stove directly on the ground improves pot stability and makes wind shielding easier.

Figure 24 – Canister Stove Options: Top-Mounted and Fuel Line

A third option is an integrated gas canister system. This consists of an integrated burner and heat exchanger that is directly attached to the bottom of a pot for optimum heat transfer. The entire unit is then mounted onto the top of a gas canister (similar to option 1). Integrated canister systems are well-shielded against wind, and their pots are often insulated to minimize heat loss. As a result, these compact units are especially efficient for boiling water. However, they can be more expensive initially, and they cannot be used with other pots.

In general, all disposable gas canister systems are easy and fast to use, as they do not require priming. They burn cleanly and reach their maximum heat very quickly, and there is little to no risk of fuel spillage. On the downside, the gas canisters are rather expensive and gauging how much fuel is left is difficult. Upright-mounted canisters have a risk of tipping over and their performance can decline in cold weather and as canisters empty and gas pressure decreases. At the least for summer trips, canister stoves are very well-suited for the WT if they contain a propane-isobutane mix. With an operating temperature limit of 21°F (-6°C) at sea level and approximately 1°F (-17°C) at 10,000 feet (3,000m) elevation, they will provide reliable heat along the trail. Liquid feed canister stoves offer additional low temperature range.

(i) Keep in mind, the fuel temperature is key not the ambient temperature. When confronted with very cold conditions, store your canister inside your tent or even at your feet in the sleeping bag to ensure the gas temperature is a few degrees above its boiling point.

Refillable Liquid Fuel Canisters

Refillable liquid fuel stoves have a similar setup to liquid feed gas canister systems. The burner is placed on the ground and connects via fuel line to the bottle fuel tank, which has a pump to pressurize the fuel and a valve to control flow. Most systems require priming, especially in cold conditions. Priming means that a few drops of fuel are placed into a dish underneath the burner and then lit. This heats the attached fuel line and causes the fuel to vaporize and press into the actual burner where it can be ignited.

Liquid fuel systems are dominated by white gas (a.k.a. naphtha). This is a highly refined fuel with little impurities, so it burns very clean. There are also multi-fuel stoves that run on white gas, kerosene, diesel, and gasoline.

Figure 25 – Liquid Fuel Stove

Generally, the greatest advantages of a (petroleum-based) liquid fuel stove are the easy international availability of its fuels, their low cost, very high heat output, and their ability to operate at low temperatures. White gas, for example, freezes at -22°F (-30°C) to which the stove is operable. Downsides are that some fuels are odorous, smoke, and may blacken pots. The stoves, especially multi-fuel versions, are rather expensive. Furthermore, flames are not as finely adjustable for simmering foods, operation (including pumping and priming) needs some practice and bears risk of flare-ups or burns, and stoves require regular maintenance to avoid clogging (all the more, the less purified the fuel is). All this requires some experience and commitment.

Regarding weight, liquid fuel systems are heavier than gas canisters due to the more complex burner and pump-valve system for the bottle tanks. In addition, commonly used pressurized gases have an approximately 5% higher energy density than petroleum fuels. However, liquid fuel tanks are reusable and can be filled as needed, whereas gas canisters can only be bought in a few sizes, making incremental adjustments to fuel supplies difficult.

Fuel Calculation

Another very important question is how much fuel to carry. For that, simply approximate how much water you will be boiling per day. A good approximation of how much fuel is needed to boil water is 0.012 ounces of fuel per ounce of water or 11.5g of fuel per liter. If certain meals require simmering after the water has boiled, add 0.035 ounces or 1g of fuel per minute of additional cooking time.

Figure 26 shows the equation with which to estimate fuel consumption. Remember to include all side trips and think about which fuel tank sizes or gas cartridges are best suited to provide sufficient energy while minimizing weight.

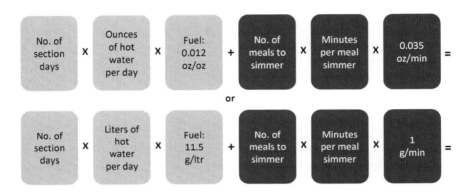

Figure 26 – Estimating Fuel Needs

Sample Scenario:

Anna is planning 10 days on the Wonderland Trail. Her estimates for hot water demand per day are as follows:

	8 oz.	for coffee in the morning
+	8 oz.	for porridge/oatmeal
+	0 oz.	for lunch
+	16 oz.	for a meal in the evening
+	8 oz.	for one cup of tea
=	40 oz.	of boiling water per day

Four of her meals each have to be simmered for 10 minutes. The rest of her meals are dehydrated/instant meals that do not require simmering. Consequently, her fuel estimate is as follows:

(10d x 40oz x 0.012oz/oz) + (4d x 10min x 0.035oz/min) = 6.4oz

So in total, Anna will need approximately 6.4 ounces (182g) of fuel for the entire trip. She can now decide if she wants to pack a large enough canister that is going to last the entire duration or if she wants to pack a smaller cartridge first and then resupply or purchase extra fuel along the way.

(i) In order to keep boiling times and wasted fuel low, always use a lid, start on a small flame and increase as water gets warmer, never turning to full throttle. Furthermore, use a screen or heat reflector around your stove and pot to shield the flame from wind.

Lastly, do not forget to bring proper means to ignite a flame. Options include gas lighters, matches, piezo igniters, and spark strikers. Opt for something that is durable, long-lasting, reliable, and water-resistant. It is not recommended to solely rely on only one option. Bring at least one backup option in case your first choice gets wet or breaks.

Pots, Pans, and Utensils

Deciding which kind of pot and/or pan to bring depends on your choice of food and on the amount of people you will be cooking for. For example, if you are cooking for 1-2 people, one pot with a capacity of approximately 32oz (0.9l) is sufficient. The more liquid the contents are, e.g., soups or water, the better the heat energy circulation and the narrower the pot's base can be. If you plan on only boiling water during a summer trip, an integrated canister system is the quickest, most efficient way of heating. However, if you intend to prepare solid meals, choose a pot or pan that has a wider base and an easy-to-clean, non-stick surface.

(i) Materials such as aluminum or titanium help save pack weight. Integrated (foldable) handles or even multi-use detachable ones are nice to have, but it is better to pay more attention to how well pots and dishes can be stored inside each other while not in use, allowing you to save additional space in your pack.

While planning your trail meals, it helps to think about and set aside the utensils it will take to prepare them. The standard minimum is usually a spoon or "spork" (spoon and fork in one) and a pocket knife. Long-handled spoons are particularly convenient when eating directly out of the freeze-dried meal pouches or the pot. If your meals require stirring or flipping on the stove, make sure your utensil is heat-resistant.

Water Treatment

As discussed earlier in the book, it is advised to treat any water along the Wonderland Trail before drinking. There are six options for doing so: micro-filter pumps, micro-filter gravity and squeeze bags, ultra-violet (UV) sterilization pens, chemical tablets/drops, and boiling. Choosing a water treatment system is just like choosing any other piece of gear – a tradeoff between features, cost, and weight. Below is a brief summary of some of the most relevant differences between the methods:

- Pump filters are fast and work well even in little, murky water, but they are rather heavy and require some maintenance.
- Gravity filters are fast and easy to use. The clean tank can double as a hydration pack, but they are expensive and rather heavy.
- Squeeze filters are fast, light, cheap, and can filter large amounts of water per cartridge (life span of over 10,000 l/cartridge). However, squeezing is strenuous, and the pouch can easily tear or puncture if squeezed too hard.
- UV lights often come as a pen or integrated in a bottle. They are light, rather fast, and can treat viruses. They rely on batteries to work and need somewhat clear water to be effective.
- Chemical options are chlorine dioxide, sodium dichloro-isocyanurate, and iodine tablets or droplets. They are very light and cheap, and can treat viruses. They are slower than other options and less effective in murky water. Plus, a slight chemical aftertaste usually remains. Also, the individual tablet dosage should match your drinking container size. Some tablets are for two liters of water and are hard to break.
- Boiling water should only be a backup option. It is slow, heavy (including the fuel needed), and leaves you with boiling water to quench your thirst in warm conditions.

Table 5 below summarizes the features and pros/cons of the different water treatment options.

Feature	Boiling	Chemical	UV Light	Squeeze	Gravity	Pump
Speed [l/min]	0.2	0.1-0.25	0.7-1.0	1.5-1.7	1.4-1.8	1.0-1.6
Weight [oz]	0.4/l	2-3	4-6	2-5	8-12	10-15
Treats Viruses	yes	yes	yes	no	no	no
Longevity [l]	n/a	80-100	>10k	>10k	1-2k	1-2k
Ease of Use	easy	very easy	easy	medium	very easy	easy
Durability	long	n/a	fair/long	fair	long	fair/long
Cost	40-50 ct/l	10-15 ct/l	$80-160	$30-50	$80-120	$80-100
Comment	Requires fuel; drinking hot water	Ineffective in murky water; wait time >0.5h; slight chemical taste	Ineffective in murky water; requires batteries / charging	Hard squeezing can lead to pouch tears; hand strength needed	Best if hung, incl. storage bags; great for groups	Pre-filter filters large particles; requires maintenance

Table 5 – Water Treatment Options

Generally, filters treat protozoa, bacteria, and particulate, and they allow instant consumption. Boiling, UV light, and chemical purifiers are effective against protozoa, bacteria, and viruses, but only if the drawn water is almost clear and after waiting a certain treatment time. All options except pumps are of limited applicability in shallow or small amounts of water. However, this, too, is not a big issue since water is plentiful along the WT route and usually very clear.

Water Storage

How to store the treated water for convenient and frequent access is worthy of consideration as well. Two options are most common: bottles and hydration reservoirs.

Practical *water bottle* sizes are 24-48oz (0.7-1.4l). Aluminum, stainless steel, and BPA-free plastic are the most used and suitable materials. Features like narrow or wide openings, sealing valves, and straws are a matter of personal preference. Insulated bottles are also available but are heavier and have less capacity. Bottle caps with loops allow attaching the bottle to the backpack with a carabiner.

Hydration reservoirs are bags made of puncture-resistant, durable material that are placed inside your backpack and typically include a drinking tube, allowing you to access the water without stopping to open up your backpack. At the end of the drinking tube is a bite valve to control the flow of water. When not in use, the mouthpiece can be clipped onto your shoulder strap or sternum strap for easy access. Typical sizes of reservoirs are 67-100oz (2-3l). Wide openings make for easy filling and cleaning of the packs. Hang loops allow the reservoir to be suspended inside the backpack.

Before hiking: If your hydration pack has a plastic taste, mix a few tablespoons of baking soda, 34 fl. oz. (1l) of warm water, and some white vinegar. Let it soak in the reservoir overnight and then rinse thoroughly.

After hiking: Clean well and keep reservoir open and as expanded as possible during storage for air circulation, or store the dry pack in the freezer to prevent bacteria from growing.

Choosing a bottle or hydration reservoir is a matter of preference. We prefer to use a hydration reservoir when hiking. Carrying 2-3 liters of water is a significant amount of weight. The reservoir allows you to keep this weight centered and close to your back, while water bottles will keep the weight off to the sides, making it more difficult to maintain left/right balance as you hike. Reservoirs also offer a hands-free drinking option and allow you to fill your drinking water only once per day rather than stopping to filter along the way. While water is plentiful along the WT, it may not always be convenient when you need it.

e. Medical & Personal Care

For lightweight enthusiasts, the following may be especially painful. It deals with bringing several items which you hope never to use. Nonetheless, a well-equipped first aid kit is essential in an emergency. Your personal kit should contain any medications you regularly take, including those that were recommended by your doctor for this specific trip. There are various well-equipped, pre-packed first aid kits available. However, hikers tend to have different needs and standards regarding personal care when outdoors. Limit yourself to the minimum you feel comfortable with. Below are some suggestions on what to pack:

First Aid – General

- Self-adhesive bandages
- Tape (sufficient for emergency and blisters)
- Antibacterial wipes/ointment
- Non-stick sterile pads
- Self-adhesive elastic bandage wrap
- Scissors or knife
- Pain relieving gels/creams (with Camphor, Menthol, Arnica)
- Anti-inflammatories and/or pain relievers (e.g., ibuprofen)
- Blister treatment (bandages, pads, etc.)
- Survival blanket (silver/insulated)
- Whistle

First Aid – Specific or Optional

- Any personal medication
- Antihistamines (to remedy allergic reactions)
- Tweezers (for splinters)
- Safety pins
- Insect-sting relief
- Sun relief (e.g., aloe vera)
- Blood thinner (e.g., aspirin)

Personal Care

- Sunscreen (SPF 30 and up) with zinc oxide
- Lip balm (with SPF)
- Toothbrush & paste
- Soap (biodegradable)
- Deodorant
- Insect repellent
- Moisturizer

! Be sure to pack plenty of insect repellant with at least 25% DEET. Many sections of the Wonderland Trail are notorious for their prolific amounts of blood-sucking insects. This is especially true in any sub-alpine meadows in bloom with wildflowers, places where the snowpack has recently melted, and near bodies of water. Devil's Dream is rumored to be so plagued with mosquitoes that we changed our itinerary at the ranger station at Golden Lakes to avoid staying there and were told by all that it was a wise decision.

f. Other Essentials

The following gear can be just as important as the gear listed earlier. Many choices are purely subject to personal preference.

Gear	Comment
Camera	The Wonderland Trail is seriously stunning. Take the best camera you have (or feel like you can carry for 93 miles) and be sure to use it. You will want those photos to prove to people back home why you did something so extraordinary. We packed our DSLR and a small travel tripod for the money shots. We also carried a small point-and-shoot for documenting moments and scenes while we were on the move and didn't feel we could spare the time or energy needed to unpack the big camera. We used 2 full batteries for our DSLR and all 4 batteries we were carrying for our point-and-shoot. Consider packing a battery charger in your cache at Longmire or Sunrise so you can recharge batteries from an electrical outlet while you are having a meal at the restaurants. Be sure to pack plenty of memory cards, too.
Compass	A compass is good to have but not essential in the summertime as trails are well-marked with few side trails to confuse you.
Fishing Gear	Mount Rainier is not known as a good fishing locale. A Washington state fishing license is not necessary if you choose to fish inside the park.
GPS Watch	GPS watches, used for running, show you exact distances traveled, speed, pace, elevation, etc. Software allows you to trace your every step back home at the computer and import data into online maps. They are useful if you enjoy monitoring these statistics but not essential for navigating on the trail.

Headlamp	Lighting in the dark is an important to think about – for camp preparations in the evenings, early or late hiking, reading in the tent, seeing your way to the toilet when nature calls at night, and investigating any strange sounds in the dark. Headlamps are great because you have both hands free. Be careful to ensure adequate battery life. Most headlamps use traditional AA or AAA batteries. Solar lamps are now available in an increasing variety, but it might be challenging to get enough sun during the day to charge your device for each night. There are also newer rechargeable models on the market that can be charged via a USB battery pack. Whichever option you choose, opt for energy efficient LED light sources and remember to keep your light handy at night.
Map	Earthwalk Press's *Mt. Rainier National Park Hiking Map and Guide*: Topographic map printed on waterproof, tear-resistant plastic, scaled at 1:50,000. The map is durable, small, and sufficient for the trail. The free Wilderness Trip Planner map provided with your permit is handy to keep in your pocket and shows mileage between major points.
Map App	Having a printed map is highly advisable, even if you plan on using an app. There are several map apps for Android and iOS. Check for recent releases. With your phone's GPS, the app can precisely locate your position on the trail. Some give additional information, e.g., elevation profile. Beware of your device's battery life – GPS services are a great drain. Cell phone coverage in Mount Rainier National Park is spotty at best.
Money	Bring some cash for food at Longmire and Sunrise, hitchhiking, postcards, emergency, etc.

Rope	Nylon parachute cord is perfect to hang clothes for drying or to replace a strap on the backpack or a shoelace. Make sure it is not too thick.
Trowel	This is necessary when nature calls. Choose one that is light but sturdy, as the ground can be rocky and tough.
Solar charger	Camps are mostly located in wooded areas making solar chargers an unreliable option.
Sunglasses	Sporty/tight fit, UV protection, polarized is a plus.
Toilet Paper	1-1.5 rolls per week. Keep a small hand sanitizer in the roll.
Towel	Quick-drying, synthetic fabric, lightweight.

Table 6 – Other Essential Gear

7. Personal Experience

In this chapter, we describe our personal experience of the Wonderland Trail, a memorable trek that we still look back on with fond memories. We discuss the logistics of planning the 12-day backpacking trip that we took in late July/early August of 2014. We offer specific details on all the stages of our planning process, from selecting our itinerary and securing a permit, to making choices about what gear and food to carry with us. Finally, we offer a day-by-day account of our remarkable journey, endeavoring to give you a sense of the trail as we experienced it. Every journey is unique, of course, but we hope that seeing the WT through our eyes will encourage you to give it a try. You won't be disappointed. We would hike it again in a heartbeat!

a. Plan

Once we committed to doing the Wonderland Trail, we were enthusiastic about tackling this demanding outdoor adventure, but we did have a few reservations. We had never hiked anywhere we needed a permit before, so we were concerned about the process of securing a permit in the lottery and wondered what we would do if our application was denied. We also worried about how to properly train to get ourselves into backpacking shape. Over the course of the hike, we would be covering 93 miles while gaining and losing over 22,000 feet in elevation. Could we become mentally and physically strong enough to do it? How would we train in pancake-flat Illinois to be properly prepared? Encountering wildlife along the trail was yet another cause for concern. Mount Rainier is bear country and has a healthy population of black bears. What would happen if we ran into a bear along the trail or, worse yet, had one visit us in the middle of the night while sleeping in our tent? Finally, we worried about the conditions we would encounter on the trail. Would there be any technical sections? Would crossing the ice fields be slippery and terrifying? Would we have to make any dangerous river crossings?

Many of our questions, of course, could not be answered before hitting the trail and experiencing the conditions for ourselves. But, before heading out to Washington state, we did as much reading and research about the trail as we could, hoping to be as prepared as possible. The knowledge we gained from reading first-hand accounts in blogs and guidebooks helped to assuage our fears and made us even more excited about the adventure to come. While we were sure there would be many challenges on the trail, the more we learned, the more confident we were that we would overcome them.

Logistics

At 93 miles, the Wonderland Trail remains our biggest backpacking trip to date. Before taking on this adventure, we wanted to make sure that it was something that we felt like we could handle. We visited many websites and read lots of blogs to get a sense of what the trail conditions would be like, what the biggest physical challenges would be, and what, if any, technical expertise would be required. After reading many first-hand accounts, it seemed that the main physical challenge would be the stamina needed for the constant changes in elevation. We were also worried about the potential for dangerous river and snow crossings, but the descriptions of the magnificence of the trail made us disregard any doubts about our abilities and got us excited to take on the challenge.

Another big concern for us was how much weight we would have to carry. Our first backpacking adventure was an 8-day trip to Patagonia, and memories of bulging backpacks, sore shoulders, and strained knees made us wary of attempting an even longer trek. We were relieved to learn about the ability to cache food at various points along the WT. This would allow us to split our food weight up into thirds and keep our overall weight to something manageable for us.

Starting Point

Once committed to doing the trail, we hoped to secure a permit, and this required getting into the nitty gritty of the logistics. In order to fill out the application, we had to decide where we wanted to start our hike and what direction we hoped to hike in. We chose to start at the White River Campground on Rainier's northeast side primarily because it provided us a convenient place to sleep the night before starting the trek and offered us a relatively safe place to leave our rental car while we were on the trail. Additionally, it was equidistant from both the Longmire and Mowich Lake food caches, making the logistics of packing food and fuel easier.

As an added bonus, starting at White River allowed us to both begin and end the experience with gorgeous sections of trail. You can either reserve a pay site at the frontcountry campground or list the White River backcountry site as your first night's site on your permit and stay for "free" (i.e., covered as part of the cost of your permit). We recommend doing the latter for several reasons. First, you'll be guaranteed a site which will take the pressure off of your first day in the park, allowing you to take care of all of your last minute logistics. Second, this particular "backcountry site" is actually located 20 yards from the paved road that runs through the middle of the campground, allowing you access to your car and the campground's amenities (flush toilets and running water). Third, you can enjoy a last supper and a cold beverage around the campfire before hitting the trail on your Wonderland adventure.

(i) The White River backcountry site is difficult to spot from the road in the campground. It is located just off the WT, directly behind the Patrol Cabin (not the Ranger Station) on your right as you are driving through the campground between Loop C and Loop D.

Direction

With a starting point selected, we needed to decide on a direction. They say that hiking the Wonderland Trail is like walking on the edge of a giant piecrust. You are constantly going up and down over the ridges of the heavily-glaciated mountain, gaining and losing over 22,000 feet in the process. It is important to decide which direction to do that in. Generally speaking, uphills are more our style, so we chose to go against the regular flow and hike counterclockwise. As 40+ year-old hikers, we generally find it kinder to our knees to tackle long uphills rather than steep downhills, especially when carrying full backpacks. With White River as our starting point, traveling counterclockwise would also give us a few easier days at the beginning of the trek to get our backpacking legs beneath us, while also saving the difficult trip over snow-covered Panhandle Gap until the very end of our journey, when we were in our best backpacking shape and most confident.

The majority of people hike clockwise, so doing the opposite would have some additional benefits. For the most part, the people we encountered on the trail would be traveling in the opposite direction, so encounters would give us a chance for valuable exchanges of information. We could receive news on the "trail telegraph" and learn about what we would be encountering in the miles ahead. While this would mean we were less likely to establish relationships with other Wonderland hikers, it also might allow us to cross paths with people we had met days earlier on the trail.

Duration

For two hikers of average fitness and backpacking experience in their mid-40s, we found that 12 days to circuit the WT was just about perfect. It allowed us to strike a good balance between the average daily distance we needed to cover and the actual time spent hiking on the trail each day. As nature photographers, we wanted the freedom to stop frequently and document the beauty of the WT, and there are quite a few side trips to waterfalls and vistas as well as a few swimming holes worth exploring. We also hoped to arrive in camp most days with enough time to relax and explore without our packs on, yet still have sufficient time to take care of camp chores (tent set up, water, cooking, clean up) in the daylight. Furthermore, a 12-day route allowed us to split the WT into three segments between caches, which meant that we only had to carry a maximum of 4 days' worth of food at a time. This way, our packs were never overloaded, cutting down on the potential for trail fatigue.

Permit

All that being said, getting our ideal Wonderland wish list was completely out of our control. No matter how we hoped to experience the 93-mile loop, we needed to secure a permit to make any of it happen. We carefully followed all of the guidelines in filling out our permit application and decided to take our chances mailing it in instead of faxing it to the Wilderness Information Center.

All of our hopes of doing the WT were dashed when we received a denial letter in the mail at the beginning of May. Of course, we were quite upset, but we had read many accounts of people successfully getting walk-up permits the day before their hikes. This was something that we had hoped to avoid, especially since it meant making a pretty big financial commitment (buying airline tickets, renting a car, and mailing food caches) with no guarantee at all that things would work out for us. When push came to shove, though, we had our hearts set on trekking the WT, and, ultimately, we didn't care where we started or which direction we went as long as we could have a minimum of 10-11 days to complete it. We decided we would take our chances, fly to Washington State, be as flexible as possible, and ultimately happy to spend two weeks hiking or backpacking elsewhere if we didn't get the permit.

With all of these unknowns, we booked our plane tickets with enough spare days to give us some wiggle room in case we had to return to the WIC several days before getting a permit. We arrived at Sea-Tac International Airport well after midnight, so we booked a hotel room right by the airport and spent a short night there. This allowed us to get up in the morning and make some stops at a few stores in the airport vicinity to get a few last-minute food items for the trail, fuel for our stove, and a 5-gallon bucket for one of our caches.

Walk-up permits become available at 1:00 PM one day before starting the trail, so we timed our arrival at Longmire's WIC for noon, hoping to be first in line on that day. When we arrived well before 1:00 PM, we were somewhat dismayed to see a group of three hikers walking out of the office, giving each other high fives, clearly celebrating some good fortune. We approached the ranger, saying we were hoping to get a backcountry permit, and she started looking through the system for us despite the fact that we were early. (Unclaimed permits are released at 10:00 AM, so, if we were trying to get a walk-up permit again, we would try to arrive then.) We started by checking to see if we could start the Wonderland Trail that day by camping in the backcountry sites at White River Campground and then proceeded with the rest of our initial itinerary request. After several minutes on the computer, she told us that everything but two of our requested camps were available, so we adjusted them to the next closest camps on the trail.

And with that, the permit was ours, and we had the rest of the day to take care of some of the final logistics before hitting the trail the next morning. We packed up a food cache in our bucket and left it at Longmire before driving to White River. We now knew when we would be finishing the trail and booked accommodation in a motel in the small town of Enumclaw on the northwest side of the park for the night we finished the trail. This was a little tough, because we waited until we arrived in Mount Rainier NP to begin researching where we could stay. Cell reception is spotty at best in the park, so this was slow-going. We knew that we would be finishing our hike on a Saturday in early August, when tourist visitation is at its peak. So even though it took a long time to find a room for that night, we felt that it was extremely important to know we had a place to stay after finishing the trail. In the future, it would be really helpful to have a list of hotel/camping options before entering the park.

Food & Resupply

Food and nutrition play a major role in planning for a multi-day backpacking trip. In addition to the suggestions in Section 5b *Food*, here are some personal remarks on the food we brought. We purchased, portioned, and re-packaged everything before leaving Chicago to save time and space. We mailed four days of food in a cache bucket to Mowich Lake several weeks ahead of time and carried the rest of the food with us on the plane.

If you plan to buy anything locally, you will have a far better selection if you stop at larger grocery and camping stores near Seattle, Portland, or Yakima than if you wait to get near Mount Rainier.

Meal	Comments
Breakfast	Our standard breakfast was an individual packet of oatmeal fortified with dried fruits and nuts or peanut butter, instant coffee from individual packets and/or tea. Our strategy was to get dressed and empty the tent, then boil water while we finished breaking camp and packing. That way, we could eat a simple breakfast and hit the trail quickly, knowing that we packed plenty of snacks to fuel us throughout the day. We also pre-hydrated for the day by drinking at least one liter of water before ever hitting the trail. This meant we had enough water for the day in our hydration reservoirs without needing to stop and filter before arriving in camp at night.
Lunch	Peanut butter in individual cups with crackers, supplemented by nuts, dried apricots, and vegan seitan jerky.
Snacks	Our snacks were energy bars, dark chocolates, and fruity sweets. We also carried a couple of chocolate bars to sustain us on longer days. We always made sure to eat something on our arrival into camp to avoid crashing before getting the camp chores done and making dinner. An afternoon coffee or hot cider in camp was always a welcome treat.
Dinner	We opted for convenience and ease of cleanup for our dinners and ate dehydrated meals each night on the trail. We also carried instant mashed potatoes for extra nourishment on our longer trail days. Powdered drink mixes added flavor to water and encouraged us to continue hydrating in camp.

Table 7 – Comments on Personal Food

Our meal plan worked fairly well in terms of quantity, although we ended up leaving the mashed potatoes in the donation boxes when we picked up our caches at Mowich Lake and Longmire. We could have reduced the amount of nuts and apricots we carried and wished we had varied the type of nuts and dried fruits. We definitely craved more variety in our breakfasts and lunches. In the future, for breakfasts we would alternate oatmeal with other options including granola and powdered milk or breakfast tortillas with rehydrated black beans. For lunches, we would alternate peanut butter with aged cheeses. We are both vegetarian so that limits our options somewhat. Tuna and salami would be good options for those who eat meat.

The following table lists the exact amount of food we packed for a single day on the WT. We carried four days' worth of food at a time before stopping to resupply.

Meal	Our Food	Quantity
Breakfast	Flavored oatmeal Raisins or dried cranberries Maple almond butter Instant coffee, tea, or cider	1 packet per person/day 1 mini box to share 1 packet to share 1 packet per person/day
Snacks	Energy bars Dark chocolate squares Fruity sweets	1 per person/day 2 per person/day ½ cup per person/day
Lunch	Peanut butter Crackers Nuts Dried apricots Vegan seitan jerky	1 individual cup per person/day 1.5 oz. per person/day 1.5 oz. per person/day 1.5 oz. per person/day 1 strip per person/day
Dinner	Dehydrated entrees	1 pouch = 2 x 11-14 oz. servings to share/day

Extra Food	Chocolate bar	1 bar per person/4-day cache
	Instant mashed potatoes	1 package (4 oz.) to share/4-day cache
	Flavored drink mix	2 packages per person/day
	Instant coffee, tea or cider	1 package per person/day

Table 8 – Personal Food Quantities

Gear

We owned all of the backpacking gear needed to hike the Wonderland Trail prior to setting out. We bought most of it for a backpacking trip to Patagonia in 2008, and, since then, we have upgraded a piece or two of our gear each year.

For this particular trip, we were generally satisfied with our basic backpacking gear before we left and chose only to upgrade a few of our clothing items and to purchase some lightweight, waterproof bags to keep our gear dry inside of our packs. Matt also needed to purchase new boots, and we invested in a small adventure medical kit.

We strongly believe that it is important to have high-quality gear, particularly when heading into the wilderness for days on end. Purchasing gear that is lightweight, durable, and built to last is a far better investment than buying cheaper items that may fail on you in the field. We always buy the best we can afford and try to upgrade as necessary. Below is an overview of our gear and some commentary on our choices:

Gear	Comments
Backpack	Our backpacks are on the heavier side at 5.5 pounds unloaded, but, even at 6+ years old, today's models of our bags are still considered to be among the best available on the market for carrying heavy loads. Rugged, durable, and well-ventilated, with a capacity of 65 (women's) and 70 (men's) liters, they have ample

	space for our gear, clothing, food, and cameras. Exterior front and side pockets and a removable top pocket are useful for storing smaller items like sunscreen, bug spray, and lip balm and also come in handy for having cold and wet weather gear quickly accessible while hiking during the day.
Tent	Our tent is a two-person, 3-season, double-walled tent that we used with a rain fly. At 5.7 pounds, it is not particularly lightweight, but we find it to be roomy and well-ventilated. We also really enjoy the covered storage for our gear offered by the two side vestibules as well as the double entrances.
Sleeping bag	We used 600-fill goose down, mummy bags rated to +10°F (women's) and +15°F (men's) with waterproof compression sacks to shrink them down for ease of packing.
Sleeping pad	We used self-inflating, insulated sleeping pads which kept us 2" off the ground. While not as comfortable as manually-inflated air pads, they fit inside our pack and were an improvement over the uncomfortable closed-cell foam pads we used in Patagonia.
Stove, fuel & lighting device	We used a liquid fuel stove that was fairly sturdy and reasonably compact. Separate refillable fuel canisters allowed us to pack only the amount of fuel needed for each segment of the WT between resupply points. We used white gas for fuel which is readily available in the U.S. at most camping stores. We carried a standard lighter and waterproof matches as a backup. We found a windscreen and heat reflector useful for conserving fuel and speeding up boil times.
Cook set & utensils	We carried only a single pot with a lid large enough to boil 4-5 cups of water. As we opted for the simplest food preparation, this was sufficient for rehydrating meals and providing hot water for coffee and tea. In addition, we carried 2 collapsible bowls and cups and 2 folding spoons to save space. One large plastic spoon was used

	for stirring and serving meals. A small pocket knife was sufficient for cutting cheese and opening packages.
Bear canister	We did not carry a bear canister as bear poles are provided in each camp for hanging your food.
Water treatment	We used a dual-action pump water filter to get safe drinking water from rivers, streams, and lakes. We also carried water purification tablets in case of emergency but never had to use them.
Hydration pack	We used a standard 2-liter hydration reservoir that fits inside a pouch in our backpacks, allowing us hands-free access to water while hiking.
Extra foldable reservoir	We carried a 2.8-liter, wide mouth, packable canteen for collecting water once we arrived in camp. We liked the convenience of gathering all the water we would need for dinner and breakfast. We could also top off our hydration reservoirs with any leftover water.
Cleaning kit	We carried a 10-liter folding bucket that allowed us to wash our dishes a safe distance away from fresh water sources. We also had a sponge and a 2 fluid oz. bottle of biodegradable soap which was more than sufficient for our 12-day trek. We used the same soap for washing our hands and faces as needed. A microfiber towel was useful for drying dishes particularly in the morning when we were eager to pack up and hit the trail.
First aid kit	We purchased a lightweight adventure medical kit sufficient for two people. We added extra ibuprofen, moleskin, antihistamine, and bandages. We also carried a silver survival blanket.
Sunscreen & lip balm	We carried a small 3 fluid oz. bottle of SPF 30 sunscreen. We always purchase sunscreen with zinc oxide to provide a physical rather than chemical barrier. We also wear wide-brimmed hats, sunglasses, neck gaiters, and long sleeves to limit sun exposure. Use lip balm with SPF liberally.

Camera	We packed our DSLR and a small travel tripod for photographing the most beautiful scenes. Whenever we got to a fabulous destination, we dropped the packs and made sure to time our snack breaks and meals with these photo shoots. We also carried a small point-and-shoot for documenting moments and scenes while we were on the move and didn't feel we could spare the time or energy needed to unpack the big camera. We used 2 full batteries for our DSLR camera and all 4 batteries we were carrying for our point-and-shoot. Consider packing a battery charger in your cache at Longmire or Sunrise so you can recharge batteries from an electrical outlet while you are having a meal at the restaurants. Camps are mostly located in wooded areas making solar chargers a risky option.
Map with elevation profile	We carried the *Mt. Rainier National Park Hiking Map and Guide* (Earthwalk Press) which shows topographic contour lines and has a useful elevation profile as well as trail mileage, camps, and other helpful information about the park to amuse you in camp at night. The free Wilderness Trip Planner map provided by the NPS fits in your pocket and is useful for determining distances between camps while out on the trail but lacks information about elevation and topography. We found it helpful to add elevation gain and loss to this map as we plotted each day's hike.
Money	We carried a credit card and a small amount of cash with us in case of emergency. We used this only at Longmire to treat ourselves to a hot breakfast and a few treats at the General Store.
Sunglasses	Ordinary, inexpensive, UV-protection sunglasses are sufficient but especially necessary for protecting your eyes when hiking over the snowfields at Sunrise, Spray Park, and Panhandle Gap.
Bathroom kit	We carried one roll of toilet paper per four days and picked up a resupply in our cache buckets at Mowich

	Lake and Longmire. We also carried a hard plastic trowel for digging cat holes while on the trail. A small bottle of hand sanitizer is useful. Baby wipes come in handy for sponge bathing.
Towel	We carried a small synthetic microfiber towel, which was useful for drying off after a swim or a sponge bath.
Headlamp	This is essential for hands-free lighting around camp and in your tent at night. We carried an extra set of batteries with us and placed a resupply in our cache buckets but did not need them.
Trekking poles	We consider lightweight carbon-fiber trekking poles to be an essential part of our backpacking kit. Ours are telescoping, twist-lock poles with anti-shock springs. We never hike without them.

Table 9 – Comments on Personal Gear

For the most part, we were happy with our gear. Everything performed and held up well. After 12 days on the trail, we only wished that everything were lighter. Before our next backpacking adventure, we will replace our tent, sleeping bags, sleeping pads, and backpacks with ultralight models to help reduce our base weight. This will allow us to continue backpacking with our camera equipment even as we get older.

b. Go

Day 1 – White River Campground to Granite Creek

Distance:	8.0 miles	Elev. Gain/Loss (ft.):	+2,600/-1,250
Duration:	4-6 hours	Difficulty Level:	moderate

With backpacks at maximum capacity and our eager legs unaccustomed to the heavy loads they would be hauling for the next twelve days, we started our first day on the Wonderland Trail with a bang. Leaving White River Campground, we faced a steep uphill climb eased by long switchbacks contouring the mountainside. This first section of trail climbed steadily up 1,600 feet over 2.1 miles through old growth forest until we finally came to an opening where a tall, slender waterfall stood sentinel to our first views of the majestic mountain we would be circumnavigating. We took in this first sighting of Rainier, unaware that there was plenty more excitement in store for us just around the bend.

Figure 27 – Hitting the Trail at White River, Waterfall on the Trail, and Snowfield above Berkeley Park

As we approached our first junction, we noticed a couple standing on the trail, motioning for us to approach cautiously. Of all the things I fretted over in planning our Wonderland adventure, ursine encounters were at the top of my list. You can imagine my delight when we finally got close enough to see that the spectacle was none other than a black bear – just off the trail. Luckily for us, the bear was quite small and paid us no attention as he foraged in the meadow looking for tasty treats. By this time, it was midday and getting rather warm. Eventually, the bear wandered into the shade of a tree just off the trail and laid down to take a nap. Despite my fears, I have to admit that seeing a bear on foot two hours into our journey was pretty exciting, and I was certainly relieved that we survived our first bear encounter without incident.

From there, we followed the relatively flat trail to Shadow Lake where we enjoyed our first trail lunch in the company of frogs, wildflowers, and reflections of the backside of Burroughs Mountain. After a quick bite, the trail took us past Sunrise Camp, over several gentle passes, and across a handful of small snowfields on the way to Frozen Lake. We followed the trail along the contour below Burroughs Mountain and then made our way slowly up to Skyscraper Peak, a short, worthy side trip off the trail where 360° views of Mt. Rainier, Mt. Baker, Grand Park, Berkley Park, and the Mt. Fremont Lookout can be had from the 7,078-foot summit. The views from the top were fantastic in all directions and worthy of breaking out our hiking tripod to try our hand at some HDR photography of the area.

Figure 28 – View from Skyscraper Peak: Mount Rainier and Grand Park

After taking in the gorgeous views, we had a pleasant downhill hike through the forest into some much-needed shade. After an hour or so, we arrived at Granite Creek, a small camp right off the trail and located close to a picturesque creek with mossy logs, rocks, and falls. Isolated and located right next to the creek, site #1 was the prime camping spot here, but, unfortunately, it was already occupied by the time we arrived.

We set up our tent in site #2, a spacious flat site with sitting logs and a convenient flat rock that served as an excellent cooking table. This was our first night of backcountry camping, and we were pretty impressed with the amenities, including an outdoor privy and bear poles for hanging our food, garbage, and toiletries. We set up our tent and made sure to hang our permit on our tent fly for any passing ranger to see. Exhausted from our first day on the trail, we headed to bed as soon as darkness fell but were startled by a large male deer with an impressive set of antlers who wandered through our camp during the night. Very cool!

Day 2 – Granite Creek to Mystic Lake

Distance:	5.5 miles	Elev. Gain/Loss (ft.):	+970/-1,165
Duration:	3-4 hours	Difficulty Level:	moderate

With only 5.5 miles to travel today, we woke up on the later side and broke down camp at a leisurely pace. We spent a little bit of time down by the creek trying to photograph the small, pretty waterfalls, but the sun was too high by the time we finally got there, making the scene too contrasty for good pictures. We had great light the night before and wished we had taken advantage of it then, but we were too exhausted when we arrived from our first day on the trail – a bird in hand, as the saying goes. We ran into several other hiking parties traveling in the opposite direction here and enjoyed hearing their words of wisdom about what we would encounter on the trail over the next several days.

We continued our pleasant downhill through the fern forest to a lookout to the Winthrop Glacier with its raging glacial run-off that becomes the west fork of the White River. Seeing a glacier up close and personal like this is mind-blowing. While the visible ice face is impressive in itself, it only hints at the massive glacier located below the rock-covered surface. From there, we passed beautiful Garda Falls at over 200 feet high and took notice of how the moist air around the falls seemed to provide the perfect conditions for monkey flower to grow.

Before long, the trail brought us all the way down to Winthrop Creek. We crossed over a log bridge, trying to keep our focus on the opposite shore to avoid becoming dizzy by the rushing, silty water below. We hiked along a ridge and through a moraine, enjoying the beautiful views of Rainier along the way. It was a steady uphill back into the forest until we reached Mystic Camp.

Figure 29 – West Fork of the White River

Because of our short mileage, we arrived at camp on the earlier side and had our pick of sites. We chose pretty site #4 and decided to spend a bit of time plotting out the mileage and elevation gains/losses we would be encountering on the rest of the trip. We were totally absorbed by what we were doing, so it was quite a surprise when Matt looked up and stated calmly, "There's a bear in our camp." I looked up from the map and couldn't believe what I was seeing. It was Day 2 on the trail, and we were already experiencing our second bear encounter. And Matt was right, the bear was in our camp – not coming to camp – but already in the camp! She was grazing in the small meadow right in front of our site, munching on the grasses and flowers, no more than 20 feet away from us. And I say she, because she had two small cubs with her!

How long had they been there? How come we did not hear them approach? We hadn't set up our tent yet, so we quickly grabbed our packs and headed back towards the trail to create a more comfortable distance between our furry friends and us. We called out to the bears to make them aware of our presence, but they were very focused on foraging and didn't pay us a bit of attention. After a while, we grew braver and pulled out our cameras to document the event before Mama Bear finally lumbered off down to the creek, cubs trailing behind her.

With a big sigh of relief, we started to set up our tent when it occurred to Matt to check out the situation on the backside of our site. Lo and behold, there was a meadow there, too. Within a few minutes, Mama Bear sauntered right back up and foraged for a bit before laying down for her afternoon nap within spitting distance of our tent. Apparently this was familiar territory for her!

Figure 30 – Mama Bear at Mystic Camp and Exploring Mystic Lake

With a sleeping bear in camp, we decided to spend the rest of the afternoon exploring the area. We took an afternoon hike to Mystic Lake and the ranger station located there, which must have the best front porch view in the whole state of Washington. We took a quick dip in the cold water for as long as we could stand it and communed with the frogs who were sunning themselves on the grassy shoreline. The rest of the day, we spent walking around the lake, exploring further along the trail, and taking in the views in the late afternoon sun. Seeing Mt. Rainier in golden light was a dream come true – a perfect ending to an exciting day!

Day 3 – Mystic Lake to Cataract Valley

Distance:	6.5 miles	Elev. Gain/Loss (ft.):	+1,855/-2,805
Duration:	4-6 hours	Difficulty Level:	moderate

We got an early rise this morning for the departure to Cataract Valley. Personally, I was eager for daybreak and was quite pleased with myself that I had managed to sleep at all during the night considering our camp-side bear encounter the day before. The morning was fairly cool, and we stopped to take some photos of the dew-covered flora around the lake before heading up to the pass below Old Desolate (7,137 ft.).

At the pass (6,000 ft.), we followed a small footpath right next to the Mystic Lake trail sign that led to a beautiful seasonal tarn where the conditions were just perfect for some unobstructed reflection shots of Rainier. Although the scene was gorgeous, it was far from peaceful. We felt like we were being eaten alive by the abundant mosquitoes in the area. We photographed for as long as we could take it and then made a quick retreat towards Moraine Park.

From the tarn, it was a steady descent through the alpine meadows of Moraine Park. The park was in full bloom and was a feast for the eyes. There were beautiful wildflowers in every direction, and we even spotted some hummingbirds and butterflies flitting about. We especially enjoyed the large patches of avalanche lilies that lined the trail for much of the hike.

Back into the forest, we were delighted to find a beautiful, geometric waterfall flowing right over the trail. The neon green moss surrounding the chute was particularly striking, and we enjoyed the cool, refreshing air provided by the flow of the frigid water. We had a quick lunch by the river near Dick Creek Camp. From there, the trail descended steeply to Carbon River along the east side of the Carbon Glacier with impressive views of the snout and the glacial river flowing out of it.

Figure 31 – Carbon Glacier and Carbon River Suspension Bridge

1.2 miles from Dick Creek, we came to the Carbon River Suspension Bridge, the first of two on our trip. Following the instructions posted at the entrance to the bridge, we took turns crossing the 205-foot-long bridge one at a time and were careful not to cause any unnecessary movement. Traversing the long, narrow wooden bridge made it easy to imagine what walking the plank of a pirate ship must be like. What a relief it was to finally reach terra firma on the other side!

From there, the trail took us through mossy, fern-filled old growth forest to Cataract Valley Camp, gaining a steep 2,000 feet of elevation in just 1.6 miles. We arrived at Cataract Valley Camp (4,620 ft.) by 4:00 PM, leaving plenty of time to relax, enjoy an afternoon coffee, and photograph the impressive specimen of coral root orchid we spotted by the group site. A creek with clean water runs through the middle of this flat and pleasant camp, making it easy to filter water. To our surprise, we were the first and only hikers in camp that night!

Day 4 – Cataract Valley via Spray Park to South Mowich River

Distance:	10.5 miles*	Elev. Gain/Loss (ft.):	+1,780/-4,195
Duration:	6-8 hours	Difficulty Level:	difficult

*Includes 0.6 miles for cache pickup

We had an early departure this morning for our biggest hiking day on the trail yet. We began with a steep and steady climb through old-growth forest to the beautiful meadows of Seattle Park. We were lucky to find the meadow in peak bloom, and the profusion of wildflowers everywhere was quite a sight. We wished we could have spent all day photographing the shooting stars, Indian paintbrush, and monkey flower in bloom, but knowing we had a long way to go and a tough hike ahead of us forced us to put the cameras away and move along quicker than we would have liked. Eventually, the meadows gave way to high alpine landscape. The flowers became more diminutive, and the views kept getting better the higher we climbed.

Before long, a barren landscape of slate rock and snowfields stretched as far as the eye could see, and we prepared ourselves for what promised to be the most challenging hiking we had encountered thus far. After passing a few small patches of snow, we traversed several large snowfields with little trouble. Luckily, the snow was soft enough to dig our boots into and wasn't slippery at all – a huge relief! The biggest challenge was spotting the cairns and painted rocks that indicated which direction we were supposed to be heading. When all else failed, we followed the footsteps of previous hikers across the snow and eventually made it to the top of Spray Park (6,800 ft.) where, despite the persistent mosquitoes that did their best to destroy the moment, we enjoyed the phenomenal views that stretched before us in all directions. We learned later from a park ranger that the mosquitoes were particularly bad here because the snow had recently melted, creating the perfect conditions for a mosquito hatch.

Figure 32 – Crossing a Snowfield in Seattle Park and Snowfield Cairn

The hike down through Spray Park was another highlight of the trek. Luck continued to be on our side, and we hit the meadows in full bloom here, too. Fields of lupine, bear grass, paintbrush, columbine, and avalanche lilies all competed for the attention of the many day hikers who ventured here from Mowich Lake. We felt like we were walking through a veritable flower factory. Despite the number of day hikers, the meadows here were a memorable sight that should not be missed!

After the meadows, the trail ducked into the forest for a long stretch of switchbacks down to Mowich Lake. We took a quick 0.2-mile side trip for our lunch at Spray Falls, where we were impressed by the very high falls that, as their name suggests, produce massive amounts of spray. Back on the trail, we bee-lined our way to Mowich Lake (4,929 ft.) to pick up our first cache at the lakeside Ranger Station. The ranger wasn't on duty at the time, so we looked in the bear box to find the bucket of food that we had mailed off earlier in the summer. We enjoyed a can of chips (oh, the little joys!) before repacking our bags with our resupply of food. Before heading back on the trail, we took advantage of the opportunity to splash our faces in the lake.

Figure 33 – Mowich Lake Ranger Station and Permanent Wooden Shelter

To get back to the Wonderland Trail, we passed through the unimpressive campground found here. This site is a converted parking lot with gravel tent pads for car campers and a small overflow area for Wonderland hikers. After four days of enjoying the relative solitude of the trail, we were happy to skip this overcrowded campsite and start making our way down the final four miles to the South Mowich River camp (2,605 ft.). Although we were exhausted, we marveled at the massive trees that dominated this pretty stretch of trail. The sign pointing to the camp was definitely a site for sore eyes, and we were intrigued to see a shelter for one of the tent sites. The group staying there seemed quite pleased with their luxurious three-sided suite.

We were the last group of hikers to arrive in camp, so we got the least desirable site (#2), but, after our longest day of hiking yet, we were too tired to care. There was little rest for the weary, and, soon after, it was time for the nightly camp chores. We set up our tent, stored our food, and filtered water, before making dinner and heading to bed after a long and hard but glorious day.

Day 5 – South Mowich River to Golden Lakes

Distance:	6.8 miles	Elev. Gain/Loss (ft.):	+2,595/-70
Duration:	3-5 hours	Difficulty Level:	moderate

We slept in after a challenging Day 4 and had a lazy departure from camp knowing we only had 6.8 miles to travel today. Much to our chagrin, that carefree feeling evaporated instantly about ten minutes down the trail when we saw the condition of the river crossing in front of us.

Six days prior, when we got our permit at Longmire, the ranger had warned us that the bridge at South Mowich was out. The level of the river here changes rapidly with the snowmelt coming from Rainier, and the bridge frequently gets washed out over the course of the summer. This is especially possible after a heavy rainfall or on a warm, sunny day when meltoff is higher than normal. Trail crews work hard to replace the bridge, but a new one typically only lasts a short while. This, of course, scared the bejesus out of me, so I was utterly relieved when I finally heard through the trail telegraph that the bridge had been replaced.

By the time we arrived that particular morning, however, the water was high and already cresting the newly-replaced log bridge in several places. Not only that, but the bridge only got us about two-thirds of the way across the river. The rest would have to be forded, and the ominous sound of boulders being rolled by the sheer force of the water had us shaking in our boots. I stood there frozen, wondering what on earth I had gotten myself into. Matt took charge and convinced me we could do it – we really didn't have another choice, right? We quickly changed into our rubber clogs, and Matt led the way. With a sturdy handrail to hold onto, crossing the bridge proved easier than fording the river's side channels, and we made it across without too much trouble. We celebrated the feat while recovering on a log nearby before changing back into our boots and hitting the trail again.

The rest of the day was rather uneventful in comparison. It was a long 3.1-mile trudge up 2,000 feet through shaded pine forest. To keep our mind off the climb, we kept our focus by counting the seemingly endless series of long switchbacks. We counted 33 in all, but don't hold us to that number – I wouldn't be surprised if we lost track somewhere along the way. We were pleasantly surprised when the trail finally leveled off, and we saw the Ranger Station at Golden Lakes (5,130 ft.), our camp for the evening. The friendly ranger allowed us to take a peek inside the cabin. Compared to our tent, it looked like a pretty cozy place to call home for a few days.

Figure 34 – Golden Lakes Ranger Station

Golden Lakes was our first time being assigned to a group site, and we were eager to see what that would mean. The site was larger than most and came with an incredible front porch view of one of the lakes. Despite its size, the whole site was assigned to us alone. Score! Golden Lakes is one of the prime campsites on the Wonderland Trail, and it can be very difficult to get a permit to stay here. We felt incredibly lucky to be some of the privileged few camping at this popular site that evening. We had a pleasant afternoon exploring the area, taking a refreshing dip in the lake, and marveling at the grand trees festooned with colorful lichen. While Matt caught up on some of his reading, I took advantage of the occasion to photograph some of the lovely flowers found around the camp.

We made our dinner up at the sunset viewpoint between sites 4 and 5 and chatted with the other hikers gathered there about their adventures on the trail thus far. Most of them were traveling in the opposite direction, so we took advantage of the opportunity and inquired about what to expect along the trail ahead. We were given lots of good advice and enjoyed the sense of camaraderie that had felt somewhat absent in the other camps we stayed in.

Figure 35 – Taking in the Sunset above Golden Lakes

Before long, it was time for the sun to set, and the crowd grew quiet in order to fully take in the glorious event. From our vantage point, the view was magnificent, and we could see all the way to the Olympic Peninsula and Puget Sound. Though a bit hazy, the sunset was brilliant – a perfect ending to yet another gratifying day on the Wonderland Trail.

Day 6 – Golden Lakes to South Puyallup River

Distance:	11.5 miles	Elev. Gain/Loss (ft.):	+2,120/-3,250
Duration:	6-8 hours	Difficulty Level:	moderate

We woke up to another beautiful sunny day this morning and prayed to the weather gods that our good fortune would continue for the rest of the trip. Until this point, the weather had been simply glorious, and we had only experienced about 5 minutes of rain in the first 5 days of our trek. How long would it last, we wondered.

Today's journey started with a gradual contour up to meadows that were filled with stalks of bear grass and blueberry bush. We were warned in camp the night before that this section of trail was prime habitat for bears, and no more than 45 minutes outside of camp, I spotted a dark brown figure on the hill just above the path. I stopped dead in my tracks and pointed the bear out to Matt. We approached cautiously, trying to get beyond it before stopping to take any photographs. This was bear #5 for us, and we were thrilled that, just like its predecessors, this one couldn't be bothered to pay us any attention on his quest for a mid-morning snack. We snapped a few pictures and moved along quickly.

Eventually, we plunged back into the forest and had a big downhill until the crossing of the North Puyallup River (3,750 ft.). Here, a sturdy bridge made crossing the rushing river a cinch, and we took some time to admire the view of the impressive waterfall from the vantage point on the other side. From there, it was a tough 2.8-mile uphill climb through overgrown bush scrub to Klapatche Park (5,515 ft.). We had to keep a careful eye on the trail here because it was difficult to see our footing. A misstep on an eroded section could lead to a tangled fall.

Figure 36 – North Puyallup River Bridge and Dense Brush

Klapatche Park is regarded as one of the most beautiful camps on the Wonderland Trail, and when we arrived, it was clear to see why. There is a small, picturesque lake located right in front of the campsites with an amazing view of Rainier just above it. Capturing the reflection of the mountain in the lake at sunset is a photograph we longed for, but, without a permit to stay at this camp for the night, we had to settle for a shot in the bright afternoon sun. Nonetheless, we enjoyed the splendid views over a quick lunch and had fun chatting with two young boys, age 11 and 14, who eagerly greeted us on our arrival into camp. They had almost completed the circuit with their father and an even younger brother. We told them how impressed we were with their accomplishment, and they beamed with pride.

Figure 37 – Klapatche Park Lake and Taking an Icy Dip in St. Andrew's Lake

After lunch, we had a steep uphill to beautiful St. Andrew's Lake (6,000 ft.), where Matt couldn't resist taking a quick dip even though the water was absolutely freezing. I wasn't so brave and opted to soak my sore feet in the frigid water while documenting the occasion. Back on the trail, our clean, refreshed feeling didn't last long. Right away, we hit another short uphill section through St. Andrew's Park with its pretty wildflowers before beginning the long descent to South Puyallup Camp. Despite having another 3.2 miles and 1,800 feet of downhill switchbacks yet to go before reaching our final destination, we made sure to stop and smell the flowers. Today's journey was just about as good as it gets as far as hiking goes, and we wanted to savor every bit of it!

We finally reached South Puyallup Camp (4,000 ft.) just before dinner time. This camp is located right next to the Puyallup River, and the sound of the rushing water provided a nice soundtrack for the evening. The sites here were sizable but more or less in view of one another. There was a very small creek on the trail to the toilet, but it was running rather dry and looked dubious. We opted to backtrack down the trail a quarter of a mile to a more promising water source, which was exactly a quarter mile longer than we wanted to walk after backpacking for 11 miles.

A trip to the privy in this camp was quite a hike, too, but it led us right past an enormous wall of impressive andesite rock formations called The Collonades. Of course, we were kicking ourselves because we left our camera back at the campsite and had to go back to get it. The rock wall is definitely worth a diversion if you are not staying at this camp, but be sure to bring your camera with you if you decide to make the side trip!

Day 7 – South Puyallup River to Pyramid Creek

Distance:	8.1 miles	Elev. Gain/Loss (ft.):	+2,850/-3,085
Duration:	4-6 hours	Difficulty Level:	moderate

We had a lazy morning in camp after an exhausting Day 6, our longest hiking day yet. We did manage to make it out of camp by 8:30 AM only to start the day with a strenuous climb up to Emerald Ridge. There was very little conversation as we both found it hard to get the legs going on this abrupt start to the day – our legs felt like they were stuffed with lead. It was wonderful to finally emerge out of the woods knowing that our big climb for the day was done!

Figure 38 – View from Emerald Ridge and Meadows in Bloom

Our mood continued to pick up when we hit the meadows of Emerald Ridge (5,600 ft.). Profuse blossoms spread as far as the eye could see, and, with a gorgeous western view of Rainier and Tahoma Glacier as the backdrop, the scene was the perfect remedy to the tough morning hike. Hiking in a counterclockwise direction, we came to a small side trail leading up to a little knoll above the main track. The vantage point from there was spectacular and definitely worth the little bit of extra effort required to reach it. We dropped our packs and took in this amazing vista over a well-deserved snack.

After taking many photographs of the jaw-dropping scene, we tackled an equally steep descent down to the engineering marvel of the Tahoma Creek Suspension Bridge. Hanging 165 feet above Tahoma Creek and stretching for a whopping 200 feet to the other side, crossing this bridge is not for the faint of heart. After convincing ourselves that there wasn't any possible way to fall off the bridge unless you were actually trying, we went for it, stopping midway to admire the amazing view. Even going one at a time, the suspended wooden walkway swayed and bounced with our weight – a little unnerving, to say the least!

From the bridge, we made our way up to Indian Henry's, taking a nice long break at the top of the uphill on a large boulder with glorious views of the western slope. A signpost at a junction in the trail pointed the way to Mirror Lakes, a short 0.7-mile side trip that the ranger at Longmire said we shouldn't miss. We ditched our heavy packs there and traveled light with only cameras and a tripod. What a treat that was! Along the way, we stopped frequently to admire and photograph the colorful meadows with Rainier in the background, and we finally got the reflection shot we had missed at Klapatche in the first of the two Mirror Lakes.

Figure 39 – Mirror Lakes and Indian Henry's Patrol Cabin

Back on the trail, we passed the Indian Henry Patrol Cabin. Built in 1915, this is the oldest cabin still in use by the park service today. From there, it was mostly downhill to Pyramid Creek Camp, a small and lightly-used camp. We had to backtrack just pass Pyramid Creek for water, but the watering hole was absolutely beautiful and worth the trip. Located right next to the trail, its clear waters emerged from mossy rocks at one end into a large, sandy-bottomed standing pool. A thick wall of salmon berry bushes served as a backdrop. The whole scene looked so inviting, but the water was icy cold. We could only stand to keep our feet submerged for a few seconds at a time!

We kept remarking how this watering hole would make one of Rainier's black bears so happy. On a hot summer day, a bear could actually sit in the cool waters while feasting on the plump salmon berries. We wondered if any Wonderland hikers have ever been lucky enough to stumble upon that scene. Water filtered, we headed back to camp and very efficiently cooked dinner, set up camp, and cleaned the dishes for an early bedtime. We had big plans in store for the next day!

Day 8 – Pyramid Creek via Longmire to Paradise River

Distance:	6.5 miles	Elev. Gain/Loss (ft.):	+1,290/-1,265
Duration:	3-5 hours	Difficulty Level:	moderate

We had an early morning departure today with a goal of skipping our standard oatmeal breakfast for the joys of civilization at Longmire (2,780 ft.). It was a quick 3 miles downhill to a hot breakfast at the Longmire Inn. A plate of scrambled eggs, hash browns, a homemade biscuit, and a hot cup of coffee never tasted so heavenly!

Longmire is one of the main visitor centers in the park, so lots of amenities and services can be found there. With a relatively easy day on the trail, we wanted to make the most of our brush with civilization. After breakfast, we had a little time to kill waiting for lunch. We checked out the different museum exhibits on the history of the park and strolled along the short, interpretive nature trail. We spotted a doe and her fawn peacefully enjoying a skunk cabbage breakfast.

After a few hours off the WT, it was time to pick up our second cache from the Wilderness Information Center. We repacked, refueled, and then re-cached a few unwanted items for the rest of the hike, knowing that we could pick them up at a later time on our drive out of the park. With only four days to go, we had a better sense of exactly how much food and fuel we would need to complete the journey. There was no sense in carrying any extra weight, so we left behind everything deemed unnecessary.

Figure 40 – Breakfast at the National Park Inn and Longmire WIC

Not wanting to let an opportunity to indulge pass us by, we hit the small grocery store at the gift shop for some cheddar cheese and cold beer. Topping that off with the can of chips we had packed in our cache, we felt like we were living the dream!

From Longmire, the Wonderland Trail parallels the main road through the woods for a while before crossing the mighty Nisqually River. After that, a gentle uphill led us along Paradise River past Carter Falls to Paradise River Camp (3,805 ft.). It was a small but pleasant camp that was very full that evening. A large hiking group occupied the group site, and the bear poles were so full that we found it challenging to find a spot to hang our food and toiletry bags.

After getting our camp chores done, we spent the rest of the afternoon lazing by the river where we spotted an American dipper in action. Watching the small bird feeding while negotiating the river's rapid currents was quite a spectacle. We read in our guidebook that we might also have the opportunity to hear or see some spotted owls in the tall canopy above the camp that night, but we weren't so lucky. Maybe next time!

Day 9 – Paradise River to Maple Creek

Distance:	7.9 miles	Elev. Gain/Loss (ft.):	+1,450/-2,035
Duration:	4-6 hours	Difficulty Level:	moderate

We awoke to a foggy morning with a heavy layer of mist and dew drenching everything. While the scene was atmospheric, it provided less than ideal packing conditions for our damp gear, and the extra water weight we were carrying due to the dew was definitely not appreciated. It was a steady uphill trek through the mystical forest to Narada Falls, a beautiful bridal veil-style falls that looked especially ethereal in the morning mist.

Back on the main trail, it was slow-going. The condensation on the vanilla leaf, ferns, and blueberry bushes proved too photogenic to pass up, and we moved at a snail's pace, stopping every few feet to snap photos of the attractive flora. After 2 miles, we finally arrived at Reflection Lake, one of the premier spots in the park to photograph reflections of Rainier, only to find that the mountain was nowhere to be seen. We stopped for a quick snack hoping to no avail that the blanket of clouds might lift. We did, however, run into a pretty doe in one of the meadows near the lake.

Back in the woods, it was a moderate downhill to Martha Falls and then a gentle ascent through pine forest to Sylvia Falls. Though pretty, both falls proved difficult to photograph. By the time we finally reached Martha Falls, the sun had come out, and the lighting on the falls was too contrasty. Sylvia Falls, on the other hand, was completely shaded and looked strangely blue in the viewfinder.

Figure 41 – Photographing Narada Falls and Relaxing at Maple Creek Camp

A short walk from the falls on a fairly level trail brought us to Maple Creek Camp (2,815 ft.). Having arrived early, we enjoyed the downtime by catching up on our journal at the nearby creek and chatting with fellow hikers.

Day 10 – Maple Creek to Indian Bar

Distance:	10.0 miles	Elev. Gain/Loss (ft.):	+3,000/-800
Duration:	4-6 hours	Difficulty Level:	moderate

From Maple Creek, the trail paralleled Stevens Creek and stayed pleasantly level as we started the last of our high mileage days on the trail. Shortly after leaving camp, we crossed the river on a sturdy bridge and stopped to admire a beautiful unnamed waterfall before tackling the gentle climb up to Box Canyon. Along the way, we caught our first glimpse of the mountain since leaving Longmire. We had missed seeing it! This gave us hope that even better views were in store for us ahead.

After arriving at Box Canyon, it was a grueling uphill slog through the forest. The trail gained 2,500 feet over 3 long miles that felt like they would never end. We looked for interesting distractions along the way to help take our mind off the climb and were relieved to finally break out of the forest and reach the Cowlitz Divide. The trail leveled off a bit and meandered through grassy meadows. An enormous flat patch in the grasses caught our attention, and we wondered what hefty animal had used this soft space as its bed the night before. We were convinced it was a bear, but a ranger we met a bit farther down the trail suspected it was more likely an elk.

As we gained altitude, the meadows became more beautiful. Impressive stands of bear grass flanked the trail with the jagged peaks of the Tatoosh Range serving as a backdrop. When we finally arrived at the high point of the trail (5,930 ft.), a thick layer of clouds had rolled in, and everything but the base of the magnificent Rainier was concealed. The trail dropped a steady 800 feet through alpine meadows where all of the usual suspects, including lupine, neon pink paintbrush, heather, and hippies on sticks (the seed pod of the western anemone and a personal favorite), were out in full force.

Figure 42 – Bear Grass & Tatoosh Range and Long Descent to Indian Bar

Eventually, we got our first glimpse of the Indian Bar Valley (5,120 ft.), an idyllic spot for one of the Wonderland's premier backcountry camps. A CCC-built shelter serves as the group site here, and there are four individual sites located across the bridge over Wauhaukaupauken Falls on a very vertical hillside overlooking the idyllic setting. By the time we arrived, only site #4 at the top of the hill was still available. We made the long slog up to the highest site and set up camp. The water source and bear pole were located at the camp's base, while the privy-with-a-view and our tent site were at the top. Between completing camp chores and trips to the toilet, we added some serious mileage and elevation gains and losses to our already long day.

Figure 43 – Bridge over Wauhaukaupauken Falls and Photo Shoot at Indian Bar Camp

We used our last few hours of daylight to explore the magnificent valley surrounding the camp. The alpine flowers were in peak bloom and made for terrific photo subjects while Rainier was still enshrouded in clouds. We explored the Indian Bar shelter, which was unoccupied for the night. This impressive stone shelter, built in the 1940s, contains wooden bunks suspended by rusty chains along the perimeter of the room. It must be fun to stay here with a group of friends and cozy up around the large stone fireplace to recount the day on the trail.

It is easy to see why Indian Bar Camp is one of the toughest backcountry permits to get on Rainier. In addition to other Wonderland hikers, you are also competing with Seattleites who use it as an ultimate weekend destination. Improve your chances of staying in this alpine paradise by timing your overnight stay on a weekday.

Day 11 – Indian Bar to Summerland

Distance:	4.5 miles	Elev. Gain/Loss (ft.):	+1,680/-860
Duration:	3-5 hours	Difficulty Level:	difficult

With a short day ahead, we decided to spend the morning retracing our steps back up the trail to a vantage point overlooking Indian Bar in hopes of photographing the spectacular scenery under better conditions. Unfortunately, we woke up to find another thick layer of clouds enshrouding Rainier. But, with large pockets of blue sky around us, we were undeterred and started the steep 800-foot climb up to the commanding view of the mountain. Unfortunately, the higher we climbed, the less likely it seemed our efforts would be rewarded. So instead, we focused our attention on an attractive patch of Indian paintbrush whose neon pink flowers called out like sirens in the thick morning mist.

Back on the trail, conditions began improving. As the sun rose higher in the sky, it started burning off the clouds, and we had a renewed sense of hope. We climbed to a vantage point and got a few shots of the beautiful scene opening up before us. Not only could we finally see Mount Rainier, but we were also fortunate to catch a glimpse of Mount St. Helens lit up by the morning sun. We lingered in the meadows and enjoyed the warmth provided by the morning sun.

After a few hours, we decided it was time to head back to camp, pack up, and move along to Summerland. While we didn't get the clear, unobstructed views that we had been hoping for, we thoroughly enjoyed exploring this beautiful portion of the trail for a few extra hours without the burden of our heavy packs. After a quick lunch, we broke camp, bid farewell to Indian Bar, and started making the arduous ascent to Panhandle Gap. The trail headed up the creek to an overlook of the valley. We followed the switchbacks through flowery meadows, enjoying occasional glacier views. Eventually, the meadows gave way to slate and volcanic rock, and the scene became increasingly impressive.

Figure 44 – Mount St. Helens and On the Trail in Ohanapecosh Park

Above tree line, we hit some of the permanent snowfields that can make this section of trail quite tricky. We were relieved to find that the snowfields were on the smaller side this year, and post-holing through the slushy snow bridges was more of a concern than slipping and sliding on ice. Along the way, we enjoyed the magnificent views of Fryingpan Glacier, Mount St. Helens, and Ohanapecosh Park where we spotted a herd of goats grazing in the distance.

After a few hours, we finally reached Panhandle Gap, which, at 6,800 feet, is the highest point on the Wonderland Trail. We crossed the saddle to look down on the Emmons Glacier, a turquoise seasonal lake, and Summerland Camp far off in the distance. The trail descended steeply at first and crossed a few more snowfields before dropping into the neon green alpine meadows of Summerland (5,940 ft.), our last backcountry camp of the trip. The area surrounding Summerland was very picturesque with pleasant meandering streams lined with monkey flower and pink heather, plump marmots frolicking about, and close up views of Rainier and Little Tahoma.

Figure 45 – View from Panhandle Gap and Summerland Super Moon

Upon our arrival, the ranger on duty greeted us, checked our permit, and warned us to be vigilant about storing our food and toiletries due to a recent bear encounter in camp. We finished our dinner and camp chores just as darkness fell and were stopped in our tracks by an enormous full moon cresting the ridge behind the camp. It seemed that we had unknowingly timed the end of our trek to coincide with a Super Moon. What incredible luck!

Day 12 – Summerland to White River Campground

Distance:	6.7 miles	Elev. Gain/Loss (ft.):	+600/-2,140
Duration:	3-4 hours	Difficulty Level:	moderate

We woke up in the wee hours of the morning to go to the bathroom. While it was still dark, we could see a tiny trail of headlamps on the mountain as climbers made their way up the Emmons Glacier to the summit of Rainier. We climbed back into the warmth of our tent to get a few more hours of sleep before our pre-dawn alarm. Summerland Camp is famous for its sunrises, so we woke up early hoping to catch some alpenglow. We braved the freezing temperatures early in the morning, but even with multiple layers on it wasn't easy.

After breakfast and breaking camp, we headed back to the meadow for a final view. Summerland is aptly named for the profuse blooms that can be found here during the summer months. On our visit in the first week of August, we found the Lewis monkey flower in peak bloom. Sprawling bushes of the pretty pink blossoms lined the moss-covered streams, making this one of the most attractive patches of wilderness we had seen on the trail.

Figure 46 – Sunrise at Summerland and Little Tahoma

Armed with our long lens, we had a chance to photograph some of the playful hoary marmots that call this meadow home. While we were there, a hiker happened to be perched on a large boulder playing a tin whistle, making the marmots in the area go nuts. We're not quite sure what their take on his serenade was, but they were definitely intrigued, to say the least! We got some great shots of the marmots posing on the rocks and enjoyed watching a family of little ones interacting with their mother.

We then found a rock of our own, where we could spend a quiet moment to take it all in and say our final goodbye to Tahoma. Just as we donned our backpacks and headed out of camp, the day hikers and trail runners started arriving in hordes. It was a Saturday, and we passed what seemed like a million hikers on our 4.1-mile descent along the Fryingpan Creek Trail until the junction where the Wonderland Trail splits off and heads back to White River Campground.

The last 2.6 miles of the trail were quieter and more like what we had grown accustomed to over the course of our 93-mile journey. We walked along enjoying our final moments of solitude in the woods. All too soon, we crossed the last set of log bridges over the White River that led us back to our car some 12 days from when we had started.

The Wonderland Trail was an incredible journey, to say the least, and a recurring thought crossed our minds over the next few days:

We walked around an entire mountain! Holy cow!!!

Appendices

A. Elevation Profiles

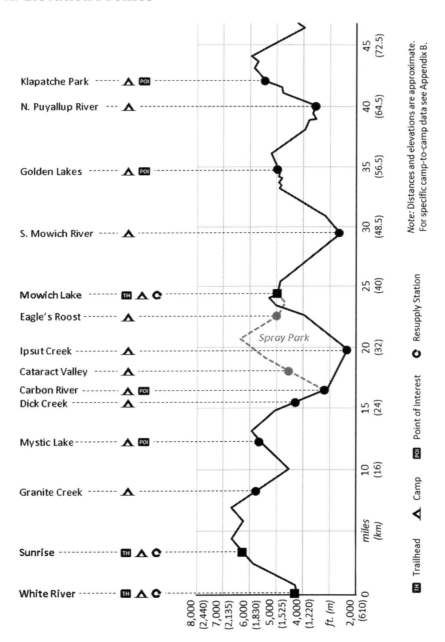

Note: Distances and elevations are approximate. For specific camp-to-camp data see Appendix B.

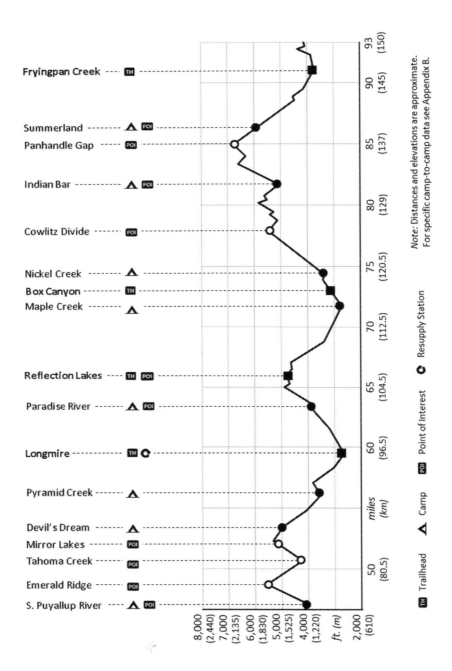

Fryingpan Creek ---- 🔲TH

Summerland -------- ⛺ POI
Panhandle Gap ----- POI

Indian Bar -------- ⛺ POI

Cowlitz Divide ----- POI

Nickel Creek ------- ⛺
Box Canyon -------- 🔲TH
Maple Creek ------- ⛺

Reflection Lakes ---- 🔲TH POI

Paradise River ----- ⛺ POI

Longmire ---------- 🔲TH 🔄

Pyramid Creek ----- ⛺

Devil's Dream ----- ⛺
Mirror Lakes ------- POI
Tahoma Creek ----- POI

Emerald Ridge ----- POI

S. Puyallup River ---- ⛺ POI

93 (150)
90 (145)
85 (137)
80 (129)
75 (120.5)
70 (112.5)
65 (104.5)
60 (96.5)
miles (km)
50 (80.5)

8,000 (2,440)
7,000 (2,135)
6,000 (1,830)
5,000 (1,525)
4,000 (1,220)
ft. (m)
2,000 (610)

Note: Distances and elevations are approximate. For specific camp-to-camp data see Appendix B.

🔄 Resupply Station

POI Point of Interest

⛺ Camp

🔲TH Trailhead

B. Consolidated Trail Overview

The below figure provides a consolidated view of the WT with regards to access roads, park entrances, trailheads, camp locations, and resupply stations.

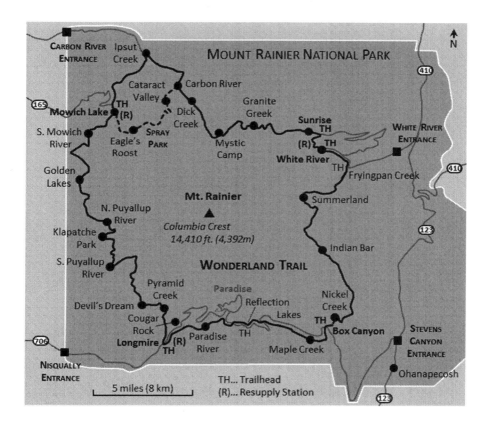

Note: The map includes four Mount Rainier NP frontcountry campsites. Mowich Lake and White River are part of the WT permit system. Cougar Rock is a short distance off the WT and requires a separate fee and reservation that can be made by visiting *http://www.recreation.gov*. The same applies to Ohanapecosh which is located in the south-east corner of the park.

C. Camp-to-Camp Distances

The following two tables are intended as a guideline for itinerary planning purposes. All distances and elevations are approximate and based on the National Park Service's Wilderness Trip Planner Map.

Counterclockwise Direction starting from White River

Camp	Distance (miles)*	Gain (feet)*	Loss (feet)*
White River Campground	-	-	-
Sunrise Camp	3.4	1,900	0
Granite Creek	4.6	800	1,200
Mystic Camp	5.5	1,100	1,200
Dick Creek	3.8	300	1,700
Carbon River**	1.1	0	990
(a) Ipsut Creek	2.9	0	795
(a) Mowich Lake	5.6	2,800	271
(b) Cataract Valley	1.6	1,505	0
(b) Eagle's Roost	4.7	1,775	1,540
(b) Mowich Lake	1.8	590	561
South Mowich River	3.4	0	2,329
Golden Lakes	6.8	2,300	0
North Puyallup River	5.0	300	1,500
Klapatche Park	2.8	1,800	0
South Puyallup River	3.7	500	1,800
Devil's Dream	6.1	2,480	1,620
Pyramid Creek	2.0	0	1,380
Longmire Trailhead	3.0	220	1,126
Paradise River	3.5	1,026	0
Maple Creek	7.9	1,054	2,054
Nickel Creek	3.6	800	200
Indian Bar	6.4	2,530	930
Summerland	4.5	1,800	900
White River Campground	6.7	500	2,100

* Distances and elevation changes measured from previous point.
** Option to continue on main trail (a) or follow Spray Park alternative route (b) which rejoins main trail at Mowich Lake.

Clockwise Direction starting from Longmire

Camp	Distance (miles)*	Gain (feet)*	Loss (feet)*
Longmire Trailhead	-	-	-
Pyramid Creek	3	1,126	220
Devil's Dream	2	1,380	0
South Puyallup River	6.1	1,620	2,480
Klapatche Park	3.7	1,800	500
North Puyallup River	2.8	0	1,800
Golden Lakes	5	1,500	300
South Mowich River	6.8	0	2,300
Mowich Lake**	3.4	2,329	0
(a) Ipsut Creek	5.6	271	2,800
(a) Carbon River	2.9	795	0
(b) Eagle's Roost	1.8	561	590
(b) Cataract Valley	4.7	1,540	1,775
(b) Carbon River	1.6	0	1,505
Dick Creek	1.1	990	0
Mystic Camp	3.8	1,700	300
Granite Creek	5.5	1,200	1,100
Sunrise Camp	4.6	1,200	800
White River Campground	3.4	0	1,900
Summerland	6.7	2,100	500
Indian Bar	4.5	900	1,800
Nickel Creek	6.4	930	2,530
Maple Creek	3.6	200	800
Paradise River	7.9	2,054	1,054
Longmire Trailhead	3.5	0	1,026

* Distances and elevation changes measured from previous point.
** Option to continue on main trail (a) or follow Spray Park alternative route (b) which rejoins main trail at Carbon River.

D. Sample Itineraries

The following sample itineraries are provided as a guide for planning your own WT route. We have created 12-, 10-, and 8-day itineraries to account for different hiking speeds (leisurely/moderate/energetic). They start from two of the WT's easiest to reach access points, Longmire and the White River Campground, and all make use of the Spray Park alternate route as we feel this stunning section of the trail should not be missed.

Counterclockwise Itineraries starting from White River

The counterclockwise itineraries more closely resemble the route we took and are designed for people who generally prefer hiking uphill to downhill, although this evens out in the end.

Camp	12 Days		10 Days		8 Days	
	Day	Miles	Day	Miles	Day	Miles
White River CG						
Sunrise Camp						
Granite Creek	1	8.0				
Mystic Camp	2	5.5	1	13.5	1	13.5
Dick Creek						
Carbon River						
(b) Cataract Valley	3	6.5				
(b) Eagle's Roost			2	11.2	2	11.2
(b) Mowich Lake						
South Mowich River	4	9.9				
Golden Lakes	5	6.8	3	12.0	3	12.0
North Puyallup River						
Klapatche Park	6	7.8	4	7.8		
South Puyallup River					4	11.5
Devil's Dream			5	9.8		
Pyramid Creek	7	11.8			5	8.1
Longmire Trailhead						
Paradise River	8	6.5	6	8.5		
Maple Creek	9	7.9			6	14.4
Nickel Creek			7	11.5		
Indian Bar	10	10.0	8	6.4	7	10.0
Summerland	11	4.5	9	4.5		
White River CG	12	6.7	10	6.7	8	11.2

Clockwise Itineraries starting from Longmire

The clockwise itineraries begin from Longmire and represent a more popular direction and starting point for the trail.

Camp	12 Days		10 Days		8 Days	
	Day	Miles	Day	Miles	Day	Miles
Longmire Trailhead						
Pyramid Creek						
Devil's Dream	1	5.0	1	5.0		
South Puyallup River	2	6.1			1	11.1
Klapatche Park	3	3.7	2	9.8		
North Puyallup River						
Golden Lakes	4	7.8	3	7.8	2	11.5
South Mowich River						
Mowich Lake						
(b) Eagle's Roost	5	12.0	4	12.0	3	12.0
(b) Cataract Valley	6	4.7				
(b) Carbon River						
Dick Creek						
Mystic Camp	7	6.5	5	11.2	4	11.2
Granite Creek						
Sunrise Camp	8	10.1	6	10.1	5	10.1
White River CG						
Summerland	9	10.1	7	10.1	6	10.1
Indian Bar	10	4.5	8	4.5		
Nickel Creek					7	10.9
Maple Creek	11	10.0	9	10.0		
Paradise River						
Longmire Trailhead	12	11.4	10	11.4	8	15.0

(i) Keep in mind that these are only samples. There are countless permutations depending on starting point, direction of travel, and pace. The above itineraries should help you gauge roughly how many miles per day you will need to hike in order to complete the WT in your desired time. To build your own custom route, check out the easy, interactive itinerary planner found at: *http://www.wonderlandguides.com*

E. Side Trips

Most people hiking the Wonderland Trail are satisfied with the 93-mile circuit. There are, however, a few possible side trips if you are a fast hiker or willing to build in some extra time on the trail. Here is a short list of some possible excursions off of the official WT:

Burroughs Mountain: This popular trail in the Sunrise area can be picked up at the junction for Frozen Lake. A strenuous 1.3-mile climb will take you to close-up views of Rainier from the First Burroughs (7,000 ft.) and the Second Burroughs (7,400 ft.). The panoramic views of the northern section of the park are breathtaking.

Mt. Fremont Lookout: As another option in the Sunrise area, this 1.3-mile trail leads to an old fire lookout with views of Rainier, Berkeley Park, and Grand Park. Look for the trail at the Frozen Lake junction.

Skyscraper Mountain: You will not regret making this short but steep 0.5-mile side trip off the trail for the incredible 360° views that come from the summit of rocky Skyscraper Mountain (7,078 ft.). The faint trail can be picked up 1.3 miles east of Granite Creek and makes an excellent spot for photography or catching the sunset if you can time it right. On a clear day, it is possible to see Mt. Baker in the distance.

Eunice Lake/Tolmie Peak Lookout: If you are staying at the Mowich Lake Campground or taking the Wonderland Trail through Ipsut Creek, a side trip to Eunice Lake and the Tolmie Peak Lookout is certainly worth your while. A strenuous 3.4-mile hike from Mowich Lake (1.8 miles if you take the Ipsut Creek route) rewards intrepid hikers with spectacular views of Rainier with a glittering Mowich Lake beneath it and a very cool old fire lookout to boot!

Mirror Lakes: Look for the signpost at a junction just before reaching Indian Henry's pointing the way to these small but pretty alpine lakes where the opportunity for capturing gorgeous reflection shots of Rainier is high. Though the first of the two lakes is only 0.7 miles off the trail, allow for plenty of time to photograph the flower-filled meadows you will pass along the way. An unmaintained trail leads on to the second of the two lakes and to more incredible views from Pyramid Peak. The ranger at Longmire told us not to miss this side trip, and we were happy we followed her advice.

Paradise: As far as seeing Mount Rainier goes, the Wonderland Trail with its 360° views of the mountain has got you covered. The one glaring omission is a visit to the Paradise area, Mount Rainier's premier attraction. If you have no plans to visit Paradise before or after your hike, you could take a detour there while on the trail. The best way to do this would be to take a zero day at Pyramid Creek and continue on the side trail to Narada Falls up to the Paradise area, where you will find an extensive network of trails taking you through gorgeous subalpine meadows to magnificent up-close views of Rainier's southern face and the Nisqually Glacier. The Skyline Trail to Panorama Point (6,800 ft.) is spectacular, but it is impossible to go wrong with any trail in this area. You can make a grand loop by following the Lakes Trail back to Reflection Lakes, where you would pick up the Wonderland Trail to take you back to camp. Mileage here varies significantly by the route you choose, but be aware that a side trip here will include significant elevation gain and loss. You could easily spend an entire day in this area, but be forewarned that you will not be alone. The sheer volume of day hikers in this extremely popular area may be a turn off for those seeking solitude.

Paradise Point Panorama

F. Checklists

These checklists are meant to assist you in your preparations. Depending on your personal preferences, you can add or remove certain items from the lists.

Clothing ( ) indicates optional items

	Hiking socks			Trail hiking shoes/boots
	Underwear			Hat or visor
	Sports bra (women)			Beanie/warm cap
( )	Shorts			Warm neck gaiter
	Zip-off hiking pants			Gloves
	Long sleeve t-shirt or button-down			Multifunctional scarf for sun protection
	Short sleeve t-shirt			Long underwear
	Lightweight fleece jacket or down jacket		( )	Ankle/leg gaiters for snow/dust
	Lightweight rain jacket			Camp shoes/flip-flops
	Lightweight rain pants			

Personal Items (optional)

	Book/e-book reader			Journal
	Notepad, pen			Tripod
	Music player, headphones			Mirror

Gear ( ) indicates optional items

	Backpack			Extra batteries & memory card(s)
	Tent/bivy/tarp			Photo ID/passport to pick up permit
	Sleeping bag			Printouts for all travel arrangements
	Sleeping pad			Map or map app
	Stove			Money
	Fuel			Trowel
	Spark striker/lighter			Sunglasses
	Waterproof matches			Toilet paper
	Pot			Towel
	Long spoon/utensils			Head lamp
	Food & snacks			Watch (rugged)
	Water treatment		( )	Rope
	Hydration pack or bottles		( )	Trekking poles
	Mug (with lid)		( )	Sleeping gear (ear plugs, inflatable pillow, etc.)
	Pocket knife		( )	Spare water container (collapsible)
	First aid kit		( )	Medication
	Silver survival blanket		( )	Deodorant
	Sunscreen (SPF 30 & up)		( )	Insect repellent
	Lip balm (with SPF)		( )	Moisturizer
	Tooth brush and paste		( )	Compass
	Soap (biodegradable)		( )	GPS watch
	Camera		( )	Solar charger

Food List per Day per Person (3 alternatives per meal)

Breakfast	
	Instant oatmeal + dried fruit + almonds
	2 cups muesli/granola + ½ cup dried milk
	Freeze-dried scrambled eggs

Lunch	
	Canned, dried, smoked meat + crackers
	Fish in a pouch with 2 slices of bread
	Peanut butter (individ. cup) and 1.5 oz. crackers

Snacks	
	Nuts and seeds
	Dried fruit
	Protein/granola bars

Dinner	
	Freeze-dried instant meal
	1½ cups quinoa, dried veggies + broth
	2 cups pasta, dried tomatoes + herbs

Other Food Items / Condiments

	Sugar		Salt & pepper
	Coffee (and creamer)		Spices & herbs
	Powdered milk		Hot/soy sauce
	Tea		Vitamins & minerals
	Hot cider		Olive oil
	Powdered drink mixes		Chocolate, fruity sweets

Resupply

	Extra food rations	( )	Celebratory treats
	Sunscreen (2oz/60g /week, min SPF 30)	( )	Clean clothing items (T-shirts, underwear, etc.)
	Toilet paper	( )	Extra batteries
	Condiments, spices, etc.	( )	Wet wipes
	Extra fuel (only if dropping off cache in person)		

G. Food Suggestions

Breakfast

- Instant oatmeal (purchase with or add flavors and sugar), porridge, semolina, and polenta with dried fruits
- Self-mixed cereals - with sesame, chia, flax, sunflower, pumpkin and other seeds; raisins and other dried fruit and berries; nuts; coconut flakes; rolled oats, shredded wheat, multi grains, etc.; mixed with dry milk, powdered soy, coconut, or almond milk, and possibly protein powder
- Pumpernickel (dark rye bread), tortilla, pita, or other dense, long-lasting breads
- Almond and peanut butter; tahini (sesame paste); chocolate spread; jelly and honey
- Freeze-dried breakfasts such as scrambled egg, hash brown, or other
- Tea bags, tea pouches (such as ginger granulate), coffee, hot chocolate, hot cider, sugar

Lunch

- Canned meat, smoked/dried sausage (e.g. traditional salami), beef and other jerkies
- Tuna and salmon in pouches; canned fish and mussels in sauces; dried salted fish and shrimp
- Hard-boiled eggs (early trail days)
- Powdered hummus (add water and olive oil)
- Crackers (wheat, whole grain, quinoa, corn); breads and tortillas
- Peanut butter
- Vegemite, pouches of olive oil and herbs; other veggie/vegan spreads
- Baked tofu (early trail days)
- Aged cheeses - repackaged in breathable material keep rather well

Snacks

- Almonds, pistachios, other nuts and seeds (no shells, with or without flavors, smoked)
- Jerky or meatless vegan seitan jerky
- Dried fruits (mango, apricot, banana, date, fig, apple, etc.) and berries; fruit leather
- Power bars and gels; protein, granola, and cereal bars; other candy and snack bars
- Sun-dried tomatoes, veggie chips, olives in oil
- Dried corn kernels for popcorn in the evening (refine with oil, salt, sugar)
- Chocolate, gummy bears, caramel bonbons (limit these "empty calories")

Dinner

- Freeze-dried instant meals in pouches (try different varieties, flavors, and brands prior)
- Pasta with sun-dried tomatoes, tomato paste, and/or pesto, olive oil and spices, parmesan
- Quinoa, millet, and couscous with herbs and spices (and dried carrots, onion, peas)
- Soup base or stock cubes, add noodles or rice and flakes of mushroom, parsley, tomato, etc.
- Ramen noodles and other instant dishes (e.g. macaroni & cheese, dried mashed potatoes)
- Burritos with rice, chicken in a pouch, powdered black beans, cheese, dried bell pepper
- Mixed lentils, beans, and chickpeas with seasoning (mind the cooking times)
- Condiments: salt, spices, little sachets of mustard, ketchup, hot sauce, soy sauce, olive oil
- Herbal tea, instant hot chocolate, hot lemon with honey, hot cider

H. Contact Information

Wilderness Camping & Climbing Permit Reservation Request:

Mount Rainier National Park
Wilderness Information Center
55210 238th Avenue East
Ashford, WA 98304-9751
Fax: +1 (360) 569-3131

[!] Reservations are not accepted until March 15th. Do not mail or fax prior to this date. Reservation requests should be submitted no later than midnight PST of March 31st to be included in the lottery. No telephone reservations are accepted!

Backcountry Walk-up Permits are issued at the following Ranger Stations:

Ranger Station	Phone Number
Longmire Wilderness Information Center at Longmire	+1 (360) 569-6575
Jackson Visitor Center at Paradise	+1 (360) 569-6571
White River Wilderness Information Center at the White River Entrance	+1 (360) 569-6670
Carbon River Ranger Station located 2.5 miles before the Carbon River Entrance	+1 (360) 829-9639

(i) Call the ranger stations to inquire about current hours. Walk-up permits are available beginning at 1:00 PM the day prior to your intended start date.

Resupply Stations to send Food Caches to:

[!] All caches must be clearly labeled with the following information in addition to the shipping label: Name of hiking group's leader, permit number, name of cache station, and exact pickup date (or date range of intended pick-up for walk-up permit). See Section 5c for details.

Longmire Wilderness Information Center [UPS, FedEx only; no U.S. Mail!]

Mount Rainier National Park
ATTN: Longmire WIC
Longmire Warehouse
Longmire, WA 98397
Phone: +1 (360) 569-6650 (Memorial Day weekend to September 30);
+1 (360) 569-6575 at all other times.

Sunrise Ranger Station or White River Campground [UPS, FedEx, U.S. Mail]

Mount Rainier National Park
ATTN: White River WIC
70002 SR 410 East
Enumclaw, WA 98022
Phone: +1 (360) 663-2425 (Sunrise); +1 (360) 569-6670 (White River)

Mowich Lake [UPS, FedEx]

Mount Rainier National Park
Carbon River Ranch Ranger Station
35415 Fairfax Forest Reserve Rd East
Carbonado, WA 98323
Phone: +1 (360) 829-9639 (Carbon River Ranch Ranger Station)

Mowich Lake [U.S. Mail]

Mount Rainier National Park
Carbon River Ranch Ranger Station
PO Box 423
Wilkeson, WA 98396
Phone: +1 (360) 829-9639 (Carbon River Ranch Ranger Station)

I. Links & References

National Park Service Website

The National Park Service's official website offers a wealth of information about visiting Mount Rainier National Park in general and hiking the Wonderland Trail in particular.

-- http://www.nps.gov/mora/planyourvisit/index.htm

Permit Application

Be sure to use the most recent, official version of the Wilderness Reservation Request Form from the NPS to reserve your camps on the WT. There is also a PDF with critical tips for getting a wilderness reservation compiled by the park rangers that everyone should read prior to applying.

-- http://www.nps.gov/mora/planyourvisit/wilderness-permit.htm

Caching Food and Fuel

Learn the ins and outs of caching food and fuel along the WT.

-- http://www.nps.gov/mora/planyourvisit/caching-food-and-fuel.htm

Trails of Mount Rainier

Comprehensive overview of all the hiking trails surrounding Mount Rainier and detailed information on backcountry camping.

-- http://www.nps.gov/mora/planyourvisit/trails-of-mount-rainier.htm

Interactive Wonderland Itinerary Planner

This interactive website from Wonderland Guides allows you to choose a starting and ending point on the WT, your hiking direction, whether or not you want to hike the Spray Park alternate, and how many days to complete the circuit. It will then give you a possible itinerary for your route. This is a definite must-visit website before filling out your permit application.

-- https://www.wonderlandguides.com/hikes/wonderland-trail/itinerary-planner/

Recreational Equipment, Inc. (REI)

REI's website offers a wide range of outdoor products and reviews as well as a comprehensive archive of expert advice for various outdoor activities.

-- *http://www.rei.com/learn/expert-advice.html*

Sadin, Paul

Very informative article summarizing the development history of the Wonderland Trail, including historical photographs and illustrations.

The Development of Mount Rainier's Wonderland Trail, 1907-1939, Columbia: The Magazine of Northwest History, Winter 1999-2000, Vol. 13, No. 4.

Asars, Tami

Authoritative guide on hiking the Wonderland Trail with detailed trail descriptions, useful backpacking advice, and different itinerary options depending on how long you want to be on the trail.

Hiking the Wonderland Trail: The Complete Guide to Mount Rainier's Premier Trail, The Mountaineers Books, 2012.

And, of course, visit

www.PlanAndGoHiking.com

for more information, pictures, and posts.

We look forward to and appreciate your feedback!

J. List of Abbreviations

$	U.S. Dollar
°C	Degree Celsius
°F	Degree Fahrenheit
CCC	Civilian Conservation Corps
ETD	Estimate of Trail Days
g	gram
k	kilo (= thousand)
kg	kilogram
km	kilometer
l	liter
m	meter
MORA	Mount Rainier National Park
NPS	National Park Service
U.S.	United States (of America)
WA	Washington
WT	Wonderland Trail

About the Authors

Matt and Alison met as under-graduates at Northwestern University in 1991. They discovered their enthusiasm for travel while living in Italy after college. As newlyweds they developed a mutual love of nature photography and have since combined this passion with international travel and a variety of outdoor activities. From trekking in Nepal to safari in Africa, from backpacking in Patagonia to canoeing in the Boundary Waters, the camera has served as a constant reminder to pause and savor the subtle beauty of nature.

Alison and Matt began their backpacking lives in Chile with a thru-hike of the "W" in Patagonia's Torres del Paine National Park. Since then, their backpacking and trekking adventures have included: Mount Fitz Roy in Argentina, the Annapurna Circuit in Nepal, the Inca Trail to Machu Picchu, the summits of Meru and Kilimanjaro in Tanzania, the Four-Pass Loop in Colorado, the Laugavegur Trail in Iceland, the Himalayas in northern India, the Cordillera Range in Peru, Borneo, and Guatemala. In the summer of 2014, they completed the 93-mile circuit of Mt. Rainier known as the Wonderland Trail. This remains one of their favorite trekking experiences to date.

While not on the road, Matt and Alison reside in Chicago. Matt teaches Latin, Greek, and Ancient History at a private high school, while Alison teaches technology at a K-8 public school. Matt and Alison document their traveling adventures and feature their photography on their blog, Take a Hike Photography: *http://www.takeahikephotography.wordpress.com.*

Special Thanks

We would like to thank Nancy Newberry, mom and mother-in-law, for encouraging our interest in photography, introducing us to scuba-diving, and sharing the trail on so many of our early hikes in the Canadian Rockies and the Maritime Provinces. Her willingness to drive anywhere and her insistence on doing three amazing activities per day lit a fire in us that still burns today.

We would also like to express our appreciation to the dedicated members of the Riverwoods Nature Photographic Society for selflessly sharing their knowledge of the camera and inspiring us to pursue our passion for nature photography.

Finally, we would like to express gratitude for all our teachers and our parents, who encouraged our education and helped us to hone our writing skills. Needless to say, all comma splices and dangling modifiers belong to us alone.

Disclaimer

The information provided in this book is accurate to the best of authors' and publisher's knowledge. However, there is no aspiration, guarantee, or claim to the correctness, completeness, and validity of any information given. Readers should be aware that internet addresses, phone numbers, mailing addresses, as well as prices, services, etc. were believed to be accurate at time of publication, but are subject to change without notice.

References are provided for informational purposes only. Neither authors nor the publisher have control over the content of websites, books, or other third party sources listed in this book and, consequently, do not accept responsibility for any content referred to herein. The mention of companies, organizations, or authorities in this book does not imply endorsement by author(s) or publisher, and vice versa.

This book is not a medical guidebook. The information and advice provided herein are merely intended as reference and explicitly not as a substitute for professional medical advice. Consult a physician to discuss whether or not your health and fitness level are appropriate for the physical activities describe in this book; especially, if you are aware of any pre-existing conditions or issues.

13763820R00098